Finding the Right Career Path

By Mary Ann Bailey

WetFeet Insider Guide

WetFeet, Inc.

The Folger Building
101 Howard Street
Suite 300
San Francisco, CA 94105

Phone: (415) 284-7900 or 1-800-926-4JOB
Fax: (415) 284-7910
Website: www.WetFeet.com

Finding the Right Career Path

By Mary Ann Bailey
ISBN: 1-58207-554-9

Photocopying Is Prohibited

Copyright 2006 WetFeet, Inc. All rights reserved. This publication is protected by the copyright laws of the United States of America. No copying in any form is permitted. It may not be reproduced, distributed, stored in a retrieval system, or transmitted in any form or by any means, in part or in whole, without the express written permission of WetFeet, Inc.

The publisher, author, and any other party involved in creation, production, delivery, or sale of this WetFeet Insider Guide make no warranty, express or implied, about the accuracy or reliability of the information found herein. To the degree you use this guide or other materials referenced herein, you do so at your own risk. The materials contained herein are general in nature and may not apply to particular factual or legal circumstances. Under no circumstances shall the publisher, author, or any other party involved in creation, production or delivery of this guide be liable to you or any other person for damages of any kind arising from access to, or use of, its content.

Table of Contents

Career Development Basics 1
Locating Your Inner Career Compass 2
The Bottom Line 5

Getting to Know You 7
Interests 9
Values 14
Personality Style 20
Thoughts, Beliefs, and Motivators 28

Getting to Know the Professional You 35
Skills 36
Talents 42
Personality Traits 45
Your Ideal Work Environment 57
Designing Your Dream Job 62

Exploring Your Career Landscape 67
Assessing Your Options 69
Places to Look 70
People to Know 72
Gathering Your Data 78

Evaluation and Decision-Making 83
Mapping Your Options. 85
Picking and Choosing 89

Getting Started 93
Developing an Action Plan. 95
Preparing for Your Job Campaign 100
Starting Your Search 106
Overcoming Common Obstacles. 110
Focus and Motivation 114

For Your Reference 119
Books. 120
Internet Resources 122
WetFeet Resources 124

Career Development Basics

Locating Your Inner Career Compass

The Bottom Line

Locating Your Inner Career Compass

Are you having trouble choosing a career path? Are you feeling overwhelmed because there are so many choices? Or are you feeling panicked because you can't find anything that really feels right to you?

Deciding on a career can be difficult, especially if you are at the beginning of your professional life. There are many different things to consider. First, what is it that you really want to do? Then, how and where do you find the information you need? How can you be sure that you will make the right decision? And what happens if you make a mistake and end up in a career you don't like?

As you think about potential career possibilities, you are most likely finding that you have a lot more questions than you do answers. As frustrating as this may be, your questions are important. Career development is the process of asking questions and gathering information so that you can best match between who you are and what you want to do with where you want to do it. The goal of this process is to enable you to find a work environment in which your interests, talents, and values are supported, nurtured, and appreciated.

Career development is not a one-time event. It is an ongoing, dynamic process, that you will most likely revisit several times throughout your life as you respond to growth and changes within yourself and within the economic and business world.

Fifty years ago, people chose one career and that was their life's work. Their only responsibility was to show up and do their job. They would be rewarded by having the opportunity to work their way up through the ranks and then retire with a good pension and heartfelt thanks from their bosses and coworkers.

Unfortunately, this kind of job stability is a thing of the past. Today's companies are in a constant state of flux with mergers, downsizing, and dissolutions. Workers can no longer depend on their companies for job security. The onus of

> Your work is to discover your work and then with all your heart give yourself to it.
> -Buddha

career development has moved from the company to the individual. In today's job market, it is the person who proactively engages in persistent career development who will secure the most rewarding and fulfilling jobs.

This book provides you with an integrated model of career development that will help you find the best career match for your skills, talents, and personality style. The model is broken into four parts: self-assessment, exploration, evaluation and decision-making, and implementation.

SELF-ASSESSMENT

Self-assessment is about self-discovery. The more you learn about yourself and what you need and want from a job, the better able you will be to recognize a good career fit for you both personally and professionally.

The second and third chapters of this book ("Getting to Know You," "Getting to Know the Professional You") will address three specific areas:

- Who you are: your interests, values, motivations, and personality style
- What skills, talents, and knowledge you have to offer
- What you want to be doing professionally and where you want to be doing it

Through the use of personal awareness exercises, peer-assessment surveys, and personality-assessment tools, this section will help you identify your skills, interests, values, talents, needs, and work styles. The information gathered through these exercises and activities will give you a clearer sense of who you are, what is important to you, and what you are looking for in a career. Having this kind of specific information will make it easier for you to begin identifying exactly what kind of career would be the most professionally rewarding and personally fulfilling for you.

EXPLORATION

Once you have some career possibilities in mind, the next step is to learn as much as you can about each one of them which you'll be doing in the third chapter, "Exploring Your Career Landscape." Through the use of different research methods, including the library, Internet, networking, and informational interviews, you will begin putting together a picture of exactly what each field is like, what a person does in each field, what the job potentials are, and so on. The goal is to collect as much information as you can, using objective facts and subjective impressions, so that you have a solid understanding of each career.

EVALUATION AND DECISION-MAKING

In the fifth chapter, you will synthesize and evaluate the information you have gathered to this point so that you can make a decision. You will compare what you have learned about who you are and what you are looking for in a career to what you have learned about the job requirements, job potential, and work environments of each of your career options. By doing this objective comparison, you will see what careers best match your needs and wants. If you have collected the right information, deciding which career to pursue will be a relatively easy task. If not, you will know what pieces of information you'll need in order to make your decision.

IMPLEMENTATION

The last step of the process is to implement your decision. The sixth chapter, "Getting Started," will focus on helping you develop a workable action plan to ensure you reach your goal. It will address issues of resistance, fear, doubt, and uncertainty as these are certain to appear in some form as you take the first steps on your new career path. It will also provide strategies and techniques to help you stay focused and motivated during the process so that you can keep yourself on track and make sure you successfully complete your journey.

The Bottom Line

Work is an integral part of our lives. At its most fundamental, work gives us the financial resources to ensure our basic needs are met. At its very best, work gives us the opportunity to take who we are and the talents we have and share them with others. Doing work we love allows us to contribute to the world in our own unique way. It nurtures our spirit, challenges our intellect, and gives us a sense of purpose and direction in our life.

But finding the right career path takes time, energy, and commitment. It is a process of asking questions, gathering information, and evaluating the answers so that you are making your decision from an informed and empowered position. It can be tempting to take shortcuts, but stay the course. This is a journey of possibilities, opportunities, and dreams, and you don't want to miss any part of the adventure.

 INSIDER TIP

In today's job market, it is the person who proactively engages in ongoing career development who will secure the most rewarding and fulfilling jobs.

Getting to Know You

Interests

Values

Personality Style

Thoughts, Beliefs, and Motivators

The first step in the journey toward choosing a career is getting to know who you are. Most of us don't really have a clear sense of who we are and what we want. Throughout our lives, we have gotten input from friends, family, and colleagues about what we should do, what we should want, and how we should live our lives.

With all those different bits of information coming at us, it can be easy to lose our true sense of self. As a result, we find ourselves making decisions and living our lives based on other people's ideas, wants, or beliefs, and oftentimes those decisions do not work out the way we planned, nor do they end up satisfying.

> **There is only one journey: going inside yourself.**
> -Rainer Marie Rilke

Choosing a career is a decision that will affect all aspects of your life, so it is extremely important that you make this decision based on what you know to be true for you and not someone else. To be able to do this, you need to be very clear on who you are and what is important to you.

The first step toward achieving this clarity is to go inside yourself and get reacquainted with the person living there. Who is this person? What are his or her interests, passions and values? What motivates her and how would she describe her personality? What are his beliefs around work and how does he define success?

This chapter provides information, exercises, and activities that will help you answer those questions. As you work through this chapter, remember the information you gather is just for yourself. You don't have to share your ideas and thoughts with anyone. So, be honest in your responses, and try not to judge yourself. This is your journey and you are the only one who knows what is right and true for you.

Interests

Our interests and passions can tell us a great deal about who we are and how we like to engage with the world, as we are drawn to participate in activities that reflect our values and personality styles. If you love climbing mountains or whitewater kayaking you probably like to challenge yourself, are comfortable taking risks, and find inspiration in nature. If you enjoy visiting museums or going to the ballet, most likely you value creativity, beauty, and serenity. If your passion is tutoring young children, you are probably nurturing, patient, and place a high value on education.

What is it that you love to do? What kind of activities do you gravitate toward in your free time? Are you particularly passionate about some activity or special cause? Some of you will be able to answer these questions with a long list of activities that you like doing. Others of you will have a more difficult time coming up with activities that you enjoy. If you find yourself struggling with your list, don't worry. This is fairly common. As the pace of our lives continues to increase, the amount of spare time we have decreases. And, if we don't have free time to pursue our interests, eventually we forget what kinds of things we once enjoyed doing.

One way to jog your memory is to think back to when you were a young child. Visualize yourself back in elementary school. What kinds of things did you like doing? What activities attracted you? Did you like playing games at recess? Or was your interest piqued during the times you got to do art, or music, or reading? What did you do after school?

Then move on to high school and ask yourself the same questions. Did your interests change? Did you notice any differences in not only how you spent your free time, but the amount of free time you had to spend? If you see that you had less discretionary time, what activities did you intentionally or unintentionally give up? Do you want to reestablish any of those lost activities?

Next, think about college. College exposes us to a myriad of new experiences. Did you acquire any new interests during this time? Were there any academic or social causes that you felt passionate about? If so, are these still important to you today?

Continue this exercise until you have brought yourself into the present. Taking the time to carefully look at each phase of your life allows you to get in touch with those activities that you once enjoyed and reevaluate their importance in your current life. Maybe you loved playing the guitar when you were in college, but once you graduated and got a job, your guitar playing got put aside. However, now as you think about it, you clearly remember the fun you had playing and the joy and contentment it brought to your life.

Another reason to take such a comprehensive look at your interests and passions is to get a more clear picture of your natural way of being in the world. As you look at your list of activities and hobbies, what can you infer about yourself? Do you like group activities or do you prefer doing things by yourself? Do you like taking risks or playing it safe? Are you someone who likes to lead or are you more comfortable following? Are you someone who needs a great deal of variety in your life, or are you more of a one-thing-at-a-time person?

The exercise on page 12 will help you clearly identify and prioritize your interests and begin to see how elements of each activity might be translated to your work environment.

Two caveats before you get started: First, make sure the interests you list are truly your own. For example, if you were raised in a family where everyone sailed, you might think you like sailing because your constant exposure to it was accompanied by the tacit message that you should like it. But now, when you examine the situation more closely, you realize you actually don't care much for sailing. Second, some of you still might be having difficulty coming up with interests. Maybe your life is so busy that there doesn't seem to be time for outside interests. Whatever the reason, you still can do this exercise. Just take some time and let yourself daydream about things you would like to do if you had the time. If you can allow your imagination free reign, it will give you the information you are looking for. And remember, the information you are gathering is solely for your use and benefit.

IDENTIFYING YOUR INTERESTS

1. In the first column of the table on the next page, list all the activities, causes, and concerns that energize you.

2. As you study your list in the first column, what common themes do you see? List these common characteristics in the second column.

3. Now prioritize your list of interests and circle your top-three choices. What do these three activities have in common? What is it about each of these that excites and motivates you? As things come to mind, jot them down in the lower section of the second column.

4. From the information gathered, list the top-three characteristics that you want to make sure are part of your job. These might include creativity, teamwork, excitement, or nature. List these characteristics in the third column. Highlight this information to ensure that you include it in your job requirements list, which will be discussed in the next chapter.

I am energized by	Common themes	I want my job to include

The information you have gathered in this exercise is the first piece to your career puzzle.

Values

Values are the beliefs and principles that are intrinsically important to you. They dictate your behavior and guide your life. Values are not something that you aspire to achieve, but the core tenets by which you live.

We get our values from several different sources. The first is our family, then our friends, teachers, colleagues, and our culture. We also can assimilate values from different experiences we have as we grow up.

As you and your life change, your values may shift. Although your core values stay fairly consistent throughout your life, events such as graduating from college, getting married, having children, or experiencing a major health crisis can cause you to re-evaluate, reprioritize, and reconnect with what is truly important to you.

Being clear on what your core values are is an essential step in the career development process. One of the biggest reasons for dissatisfaction and conflict, in both our personal and professional lives, occurs when we are living in opposition to our core values.

For example, if you value health and well-being, working for a company that requires 50- to 60-hour work weeks would not be a good match. And if you place a high value on excellence, working in a job that only requires mediocre quality would be frustrating for you.

Oftentimes, people try to repress or ignore what they know their values to be in order to fit into a certain environment. This approach may seem to work, but sooner or later the disparity between what you truly believe and how you are living your life will begin to cause friction. Your values are the guiding principals of your life. It is important that you recognize and honor them.

The goal of the exercise on the following page is to help you identify your values. The exercise is broken into three parts. The first part will ask you to identify the values that are most important to you. These can be called your core values.

The second part will ask you to identify what values are important in a work environment. These values may not hold the same priority as your core values, but they will influence your career and job choices.

Once you've identified your two sets of values, compare them to see where commonalities lie between your personal and work values, as well as any potential conflicts.

IDENTIFYING YOUR CORE VALUES, PART I

Review the list below and circle the ten values that you feel are most important in guiding your life. Feel free to add values that are not on the list but are nonetheless important to you. Once you have your list of ten, number them to rank their importance, with one being the most important.

Values List A

Accomplishment	Fairness	Practicality
Achievement	Family	Privacy
Adventure	Friendship	Quality
Autonomy	Fun/laughter	Recognition
Beauty	Generosity	Reliability
Calm	Goodness	Respect
Challenge	Gratitude	Responsibility
Change	Hard work	Safety
Commitment	Health/well-being	Self-reliance
Competence	Honor	Simplicity
Decisiveness	Humor	Status
Determination	Integrity	Structure
Dignity	Joy	Teamwork
Discipline	Justice	Tolerance
Diversity	Knowledge	Tradition
Efficiency	Leadership	Trust
Excellence	Loyalty	Wealth
Equality	Perfection	Wisdom

Other _____

_____

_____

IDENTIFYING YOUR CORE VALUES, PART I

Now go back through the list and cross out three of the values you circled. As you review your list you may want to re-rank it.

Go through the list one more time and cross out two more of the values. Now you are left with your top-five values.

Review your remaining top-five values and make sure that you are comfortable with them. Feel free to exchange any of the values for others that you have eliminated, or for values that may have just occurred to you. The object is to make sure that the list you have represents your true top-five values.

Now prioritize your final five and list them below.

My Core Values

1. _____
2. _____
3. _____
4. _____
5. _____

IDENTIFYING YOUR CORE VALUES, PART II

Below is a list of values that describe a variety of attributes associated with work environments. Go through the list and circle the five that are most important to you. It might be helpful to go through the entire list and rank each value with a one, two, or three, with one being the most important.

If you end up with more than five "ones," review your list and choose your true top-five values. If you don't have enough "ones," go back to your "twos" and think about which of those you want to add to your list of five key work values.

Values List B

Accomplishment	Flexibility	Personal growth
Advancement	Freedom	Physical work
Adventure	Fun	Power
Aesthetics	Help society	Prestige
Autonomy	Independence	Problem solving
Competition	Influence	Recognition
Cooperation	Integrity	Routine work
Creativity	Intellectual stimulation	Stability/security
Education/learning	Leadership	Teamwork
Equality	Leisure	Tolerance
Excitement	Location	Travel
Fast pace	Moral fulfillment	Variety

Other _____

_____

_____

IDENTIFYING YOUR CORE VALUES, PART II

My Core Work Values

1. _____
2. _____
3. _____
4. _____
5. _____

Now review your two lists of values. You might see that you have put one or more values that are similar on both lists, or that your lists have different values, but are complementary. For instance, integrity, excellence, independence, creativity, and respect are values that could easily be placed on either list.

You might also notice that some values on your lists might be in conflict. For example, if family and well-being are on your core value list, and travel and fast pace are on your work list, there is a potential for problems if you allow the work-life balance to become unsteady. This doesn't mean that it's not possible to allow for both sets of values. It will just take a little more awareness on your part to stay ahead of potential conflicts.

Our values flow through every aspect of our lives. They are reflected in our goals, our relationships, our commitments, and our careers. Having a greater understanding of your values and how they affect your workplace priorities will greatly strengthen your ability to choose a satisfying and rewarding career.

Personality Style

Our personalities comprise all our individual qualities—attitudes, behaviors, and emotions. Everyone is born with their own unique combination of these characteristics, giving each person a distinct personality and way of acting and responding to the world.

For centuries, people have been trying to categorize these different response patterns into personality styles in order to help people better understand how they, and others, interact with the world. Today there are many personality assessment instruments available, such as the Myers-Briggs Trait Inventory, Holland's Personality Types, Keirsey Temperament Sorter, the Strong Interest Inventory®, and the Enneagram to help you gain a sense of who you are and how you interact with the world. Becoming more aware of your individual personality style will make it easier for you to choose career options that will fit your needs and interests.

This section will discuss two of the most popular assessment instruments, Holland's Personality Types and the Myers-Briggs Trait Inventory. The information presented in this section is just a brief overview of each assessment tool, intended to introduce you to the basic concepts of each. If you are interested in learning more about personality assessment tools, please refer to the "For Your Reference" chapter in the back of this book.

HOLLAND'S PERSONALITY TYPES

Dr. John Holland, professor emeritus at Johns Hopkins University, is a psychologist who devoted his professional life to researching issues related to career choice and satisfaction. He developed what has become a well-known theory, Holland's personality-type career-development theory, and designed several assessments and supporting materials to assist people in making effective career choices.

At the beginning of his career Holland was a classifications interviewer with the army, and it was there, through his experience interviewing army personnel, that he began to see how people naturally fall into distinct personality types. He took this information and developed Holland's personality-type career-development theory, which today is the best-known and most widely researched theory on the topic of career choice.

Holland's theory states that:

- In our culture, most people fall into one of six personality types. These are realistic, investigative, artistic, social, enterprising, and conventional.

- People with the same personality type tend to be attracted to each other. For example, enterprising people are more likely to make friends and work with other enterprising people.

- There are also six basic types of work environments. These are realistic, investigative, artistic, social, enterprising, and conventional.

- People who choose to work in an environment that matches their personality type are more likely to be successful and happy in their work.

- How you act and feel at work depends on your workplace environment. If you are working with people who have a similar personality type as yours, your skills and interests will be more valued and you will feel more comfortable in your work environment.

Holland's research also found that, although most people relate to one dominant type, they also can see similarities within the two compatible personality types, meaning that they share aspects with these other types. According to Holland's theory, someone seeking the greatest probability of being satisfied in a career should choose an occupation that matches his or her type (dominant) or is similar to his or her type (compatible).

Dominant Type	Compatible Types
realistic	investigative, conventional
investigative	realistic, artistic
artistic	investigative, social
social	artistic, enterprising
enterprising	social, conventional
conventional	enterprising, realistic

Below are the descriptions of each personality type and a list of related occupations. As you read the descriptions, keep in mind that you will probably relate to more than one type. Also, be honest in your self-assessment. Which of these types truly describes your personality and interests? Try not to fall into the trap of choosing a type because it's what you think you should be.

Holland's Personality Types

Realistic: People in this category generally like practical activities that require mechanical skills or physical coordination. They like athletic and outdoor activities, and they enjoy working with their hands using machines or tools. They can be described as practical, honest, quiet, shy, genuine, and humble.

Related occupations: aircraft controller, surveyor, electrician, engineer, mechanic, tradesman

Investigative: People in this category like to explore and understand things or events. They can be described as analytical, cautious, curious, independent, intellectual, introverted, rational, methodical, and precise.

Related occupations: biologist, chemist, geologist, medical technician, laboratory assistant

Artistic: People in this category like to work with creative ideas and self-expression more than routines and rules. They can be described as complicated, disorderly, emotional, expressive, imaginative, nonconforming, impulsive, and introspective.

Related occupations: composer, musician, actor, designer, writer, dancer

Social: People in this category like to help, teach, train, heal, and counsel people. They can be described as friendly, cooperative, helpful, idealistic, patient, kind, warm, and understanding.

Related occupations: teacher, counselor, nurse, minister, social worker

Enterprising: People in this category like to persuade or direct people. They enjoy planning projects and organizing people to achieve group goals. They can be described as adventuresome, ambitious, energetic, extroverted, self-confident, and social.

Related occupations: business executive, salesperson, supervisor, manager, travel agent

Conventional: People in this category like to follow orderly routines and meet clear standards. They prefer structure and order, enjoy bringing closure to situations, and have clerical and mathematic abilities. They can be described as conscientious, conforming, orderly, obedient, practical, and persistent.

Related occupations: financial analyst, bookkeeper, tax expert, banker, radio dispatcher, entrerpreneur, consultant

Which type, or types, best describe you?

1. _____

2. _____

3. _____

A key part of Holland's theory states that people are the happiest and most successful when they are working in environments that can support and nurture their individual personality type.

What type of work environments do you feel would best match your personality type?

1. _____

2. _____

3. _____

Without a clear sense of who you are and what you want, it can be easy to find yourself working in a field that is not a good fit for your personality or interests. Family pressure, the lure of financial reward, and the confusion of not really knowing what you want can cause you to choose jobs that are not personally satisfying or rewarding.

Using proven tools such as the Holland Personality Type Inventory can help you become certain about your individual interests and personality style, and enable you to make more informed and productive decisions regarding your career. For more in-depth information on Holland's Inventory see the "For Your Reference" section in the back of this book.

MYERS-BRIGGS TRAIT INVENTORY (MBTI)

One of the most widely used assessment tools for identifying personality types and working styles is the Myers-Briggs Trait Inventory. The MBTI was developed by Katherine Briggs and her daughter, Isabel Briggs-Myers, in the 1940s to make C.G. Jung's theory of human personality more understandable and useful in everyday life.

Jung identified eight types of mental processes or ways of relating to the world. Myers and Briggs took Jung's eight types of mental processes and broke them into four categories. They then developed a written exercise to indicate what a person's dominant, or preferred, way of relating to the world is in each of the four categories. Descriptions of the four categories follow.

Energy

Where do you prefer to direct your energy?

- **Extraversion (E):** You tend to focus on the outer world of people and things.
- **Introversion (I):** You tend to focus on the inner world of ideas, information, and impressions.

Information

How do you prefer to process information?

- **Sensing (S):** You tend to focus on the present and on concrete information gained by your senses.
- **Intuitive (N):** You tend to focus on the future with a view of patterns and possibilities.

Decisions

How do you prefer to make decisions?

- **Thinking (T):** You tend to base your decisions on logic and on objective analysis of cause and effect.
- **Feeling (F):** You tend to base your decisions on values and personal beliefs as to what you feel to be important.

Organization

How do you prefer to organize your life?

- **Judging (J):** You like a planned and organized approach to life. (Please note that judging is not the same as judgmental.)
- **Perceiving (P):** You like a flexible and spontaneous approach to life and prefer to keep your options open.

The Myers-Briggs Trait Inventory asserts that each of us has a natural preference in all of the categories. We are primarily extraverted or introverted, sensing or intuitive, thinking or feeling, and judging or perceiving.

A good analogy is your tendency to use one hand instead of the other. You have two hands and are able to use them both, but you have a natural inclination to be either left-handed or right-handed. Similarly, you have many facets to your personality and you use all of them at one time or another. But you have preferences, specific ways in which you feel most comfortable relating to the world.

The MBTI uses four-letter codes to identify the 16 possible personality types, with each type having its own unique set of characteristics. Below are brief descriptions of four sample personality types. Notice the difference in the preferred way of relating to the world.

ISTJ (Introversion, Sensing, Thinking, and Judging): ISTJs are described as people who are logical, pay a lot of attention to detail, are committed, and who have a deep sense of responsibility. They are practical, realistic, and value tradition and loyalty.

ESFP (Extroversion, Sensing, Feeling, and Perceiving): ESFPs are described as caring, warm people who love life. They are energetic, flexible, spontaneous, and love to be involved with new activities. They enjoy working with others to make things happen.

ENFJ (Extroversion, Intuitive, Feeling, and Judging): ENFJs are described as sociable, empathic, and responsible. They are highly attuned to the emotions and needs of others and enjoy helping people fulfill their potential. They are loyal individuals who can provide inspiring leadership.

INTP (Introversion, Intuitive, Thinking, Perceiving): INTPs are analytical and often skeptical. They seek to develop logical explanations for everything that interests them. They are quiet, contained, flexible, and adaptable, and they have an unusually strong ability to focus in-depth and solve problems in their areas of interest.

Try these online resources for descriptions of the other personality combinations:

TypeLogic (www.typelogic.com)
The Personality Page (www.personalitypage.com/high-level.html)

Though many factors combine to influence an individual's behaviors, values, and attitudes, the four-letter descriptions summarize underlying patterns and behaviors common to most people of that type. The results of the MBTI offer insight and understanding of personalities, and can help you choose what kind of job tasks and work environments would best suit your personality type. The resulting information will also increase your understanding of why certain people and situations always seem to present challenges for you.

With this knowledge you will be more aware of how much a potential job will allow you to use your natural strengths and how often you might be called upon to use your less dominant behaviors, enabling you to make a conscious decision regarding what level of challenge you want, or are willing, to take at this point in your career.

Career development is a journey of constant self-assessment and the Myers-Briggs Trait Inventory is a great first step in this process. For more information on the MBTI, see the "For Your Reference" chapter in the back of this book.

Self-assessment tools can give you a great deal of valuable information about how you operate in the world. They are also useful in helping you see that there are many different ways to be in the world and that not everyone perceives the world the same way you do.

Although there is an underlying belief that all people are, or should be, the same, the bottom line is that people are different from each other. We want different things. We have different goals, values, and needs. We believe differently. We think, perceive, and communicate differently. And therefore, we all need to find a career that best fits our individual characteristics. When it comes to careers, one size does not fit all.

Embrace who you are, including all your strengths, weaknesses, and individual quirks; and give yourself permission to seek out a career that will truly match your style, needs, and interests.

Thoughts, Beliefs, and Motivators

THOUGHTS AND BELIEFS

One of the most important parts of self-discovery is taking the time to examine the beliefs and stories you have integrated into your self-perception and worldview that may be holding you back from achieving your goals and dreams.

One of the biggest obstacles people face when they are trying to make any kind of life change, whether it is deciding on a new career or buying a new house, is self-defeating thoughts. These are the thoughts that say you are not smart enough, you don't work hard enough, or that you should be more successful. These are the thoughts that are very often preceded by the word *should*, and keep you focused on what you think is the right and acceptable thing to do versus what you truly want to do.

These thoughts can be incredibly powerful, and you may have already noticed that the closer you get to making a decision, the louder the voices become. When you give up, or back down, the voices appear to lessen in intensity. That is why so many people throw in the towel before they reach their goal. They can't tolerate the fear, discomfort, and anxiety that these thoughts produce. Unfortunately, that leaves them living a life that is less than their ideal and always wondering what would have happened if. . . .

As you begin exploring different career options, it will be very important for you to be aware of any sabotaging thoughts and myths that might be skewing your perspective. A good place to start is noticing the kind of language you use as you debate the pros and cons of different careers. How often do you use negative or judgmental words? How often does the word *should* appear?

> **The world is full of people who have stopped listening to themselves or have listened only to their neighbors to learn what they ought to do, how they ought to behave, and what the values are that they should be living for.**
> **—Joseph Campbell**

The key here is to just notice the critical voices. Try not to be judgmental about them, but rather, gently ask yourself whose voice is really making the statement? If you can identify the source, give the statement back to that person and replace it with a statement of your own that speaks from your heart and that validates who you know yourself to be.

Draw from the below examples.

Critical statement: I would love to be a financial planner, but I am really stupid when it comes to math, so I could never make it through the training.

Whose voice? 4th grade math teacher.

Your statement: I would love to be a financial planner. I know that I sometimes have a little trouble with math, so I'll just hire a tutor to help me when I need it.

Critical statement: I really should be looking at a more sensible career. Any idiot knows you can't make a living by being a dancer.

Whose voice? My father.

Your statement: I love to dance and I want to pursue it as a career. I know it will probably take a while to start making a living at it, so I will probably have to get a part-time job in the interim.

The next thing to pay attention to is how much validity you give your thoughts. In reality, thoughts are just thoughts. It is only when we start to believe them and attach meaning to them that we get into trouble. So, when you notice yourself having a self-critical thought, challenge its validity. How do you know that it is the honest truth? Just because we have been conditioned to believe something does not make it true.

Susan is a very talented artist. She always dreamed about making art her life work, but she was raised with the beliefs that art is a hobby and to be a responsible person, one had to have a "real" job. Susan worked in the "real" world for years, doing her art on the side. Although she was good at her job, she never stopped thinking about being a full-time artist. Yet her beliefs about what it meant to be responsible kept holding her back from going for her dream.

After battling her thoughts about what she thought she "should" do and what she knew she wanted to do, Susan finally took a leap of faith to follow her heart. She quit her job, moved her family to a quiet place in the country, and began painting full time. She and her family love the slower-paced lifestyle of the country, and Susan has been very successful in selling her paintings in art shows throughout the area. She now describes herself as a happy, productive, and responsible member of her community.

What are some of your tightly held beliefs around work, careers, and your abilities that might get in the way of you pursuing your desired career? The following exercise will help you begin to separate your thoughts and beliefs from those that you have assimilated from family, friends, and society.

IDENTIFYING YOUR BELIEFS

Below are some typical career-related questions. Pull out a sheet of paper (or a Word document), answer each question, and set your answers aside.

1. How do you define success?

2. What role do you want work to play in your life?

3. What do you see as your strengths?

4. What do you see as your weaknesses?

5. Where are you getting your information regarding your strengths and weaknesses?

6. What kinds of careers do you feel would be best for you to pursue? Why?

7. What kinds of careers interest you the most? Why?

8. In making a career decision, will you be more likely to follow your intellect or your heart? Why?

9. What obstacles do you see standing between you and your career of choice, that is, skills, education, age, gender, minority status, and so on? Be specific.

10. How real are these obstacles and what steps can you take to lessen or eliminate them?

After a day or two, go back to the questions and carefully think about each of your answers. Do your answers truly reflect your thoughts and beliefs or do parts of them belong to other people?

Often we answer these kinds of questions without really thinking about what we want to say, but rather what we think we should say. Revise your answers as needed to make sure that they are congruous with what *you* believe.

MOTIVATORS

Motivation plays a large part in a person's ability to be successful in his or her personal and professional lives. Motivation is what impels us to take action. Motivation helps us overcome obstacles and break through resistance. And motivation is what gives us the ability to stay focused and keep moving toward our goals.

Most of us can tell when we are feeling motivated and when we are not. But how many of us can clearly identify the specific factors that cause us to feel good about what we are doing and that compel us to keep moving forward? Knowing what motivates you is a key piece to your career puzzle. Everyone has their own set of motivators. Unless you are clear about what your driving forces are, you could easily end up in a work environment that doesn't motivate you. And without motivation, it is very difficult to maintain any enthusiasm for and dedication to your job.

For example, if you are motivated by camaraderie and interaction with other people, working in an environment in which there is little or no opportunity for interacting will eventually stifle your energy and enthusiasm. Or if you are motivated by large financial gains, working for a small nonprofit organization would probably not be a good choice for you.

WHAT MOTIVATES YOU?

Following is a partial list of motivators. Which ones are important to you?

- Achievement
- Beauty/aesthetics
- Challenges/problem solving
- Desire to be loved
- Desire to contribute to the greater good
- Fame
- Fortune
- Intellectual growth
- Personal fulfillment
- Recognition
- Social interaction/camaraderie
- Others _____

_____

_____

WHAT MOTIVATES YOU?, CONT'D

As you think about what motivates you, be sure to ask yourself if the motivators you have chosen are truly yours. Once again, it can be easy to select the things that you think you *should* be motivated by, such as money and achievement. You might actually be much more energized by beauty and personal fulfillment, but not consciously aware of it. Motivation plays an important role in the success and happiness of your life, so be honest with yourself.

My Top Three Motivators

1. _____

2. _____

3. _____

The last four sections have given you many pieces to your career puzzle. You have identified your interests, your personal and work values, and are more aware of your personality type. You have challenged some of your outdated thoughts and beliefs, and you have a better sense of what kinds of things motivate you. You have begun to reconnect with who you are and what you need and want to ensure your professional success and personal fulfillment. In the next chapter, the journey will continue as you take an in-depth look at your skills, talents, and abilities.

Getting to Know the Professional You

Skills

Talents

Personality Traits

Your Ideal Work Environment

Designing Your Dream Job

A common barrier to finding fulfilling and rewarding work is the inability to clearly articulate what skills and strengths you have to offer future employers. In this chapter you will identify your unique combination of skills, talents, and personality traits and prioritize which ones you want to use, strengthen, or develop. You will also find tips to help you to talk more clearly, comfortably, and confidently about the strengths you have and how to present those to employers.

Skills

It can be tempting to take a job or follow a career path because it feels comfortable to you. You may decide to accept a job offer because it requires skills you have, even though you no longer enjoy using these particular skills. But somehow you get lulled into the comfort of the familiar, and before long you find yourself bored, then frustrated, and eventually burned out.

Luckily, there are steps you can take to avoid this trap. One of the most effective things you can do is to complete a personal and professional skills inventory. This will help you clearly identify the skills you have, the skills you like using, and the skills you want to continue developing.

But before you get started, it is important to have a clear definition of what a skill really is. *Merriam-Webster* defines a skill as "a learned power of doing something competently: a developed aptitude or ability." Skills are abilities acquired through study, training, and practice. Skills are different from talents, which are natural abilities. In the next section you will have the chance to inventory your skills.

SKILLS INVENTORY

The purpose of the skills inventory is to create a comprehensive list of your skills. To ensure that you don't forget to include skills that you are not currently using, or skills that are now so ingrained that they feel more like second-nature, it works best to break the inventory into four sections.

In the first section, "Education/Training Skills," include any skills that you have learned through school or special training programs. These may include skills in the areas of computers, accounting, writing, and graphic design.

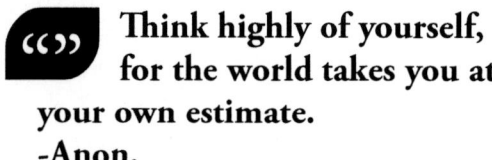

Think highly of yourself, for the world takes you at your own estimate.
-Anon.

In the second section, "Work Skills," include all the skills you have learned from your previous jobs. Think about all the jobs you have held, whether they were full- or part-time and list the skills you acquired from each. These might include creating budgets, program development, specific computer programs, and presentation skills.

In the next section, "Volunteer Skills," list the skills you have learned through any type of community activity. These could include community relations, fund development, public relations, mentoring, or tutoring skills.

In the last section, "Leisure/Fun Skills," list the skills you have acquired through your hobbies and outside interests. This list might include teamwork, mediation, motivation, and goal setting.

To be most effective, this inventory should be as inclusive as possible, so take the time you need to prepare a complete list. You do not need to finish this exercise in a single sitting. It might be useful to put it aside and revisit it after a few days to see if any other skills come to mind.

Education/Training Skills

Work Skills

Volunteer Skills

Leisure/Fun Skills

SKILL TYPES

Most of the skills we have can be divided into three categories: people, information/ideas, and things. Below are some typical types of skills associated with each category.

People	Information/Ideas	Things
Mentoring	Analyzing	Precision working
Coaching	Evaluating	Restoring
Consulting	Creating	Operating machines
Supervising	Examining	Installing
Managing	Testing	Constructing
Teaching	Computing	Using your hands
Negotiating	Problem Solving	Remodeling

As you look through your skills inventory, do you see any patterns? Are your skills more related to working with people, ideas, or things? You might have skills that fall into all three categories, but one area will probably dominate. Being aware of your dominant category will enable you to choose a work environment that will best support and nurture your specific skill set.

TOP-FIVE SKILLS

Review your skills inventory one more time. As you look through your skills, cross out the five that you no longer have any desire to use. Maybe you had a job that required you to develop your grant-writing skills. Even though you became highly competent at it, you really don't like doing it. Crossing off these skills will be a reminder to you not to take a job that requires these skills—even if the job seems like a good idea at the time.

Next, circle your top-five skills. These are the skills you love using and want to continue to develop. Once you have your five, prioritize them in order of what is most important to you. These are the skills that you want to make sure are part of your career. To ensure that happens, you will need to be able to talk about these skills in a confident and knowledgeable manner. The exercise on the following page will help you with that process.

ASSESSING YOUR TOP-FIVE SKILLS

Consider your top-five skill priorities and answer the following questions for each:

Where did you learn this skill?

1) _____

2) _____

3) _____

4) _____

5) _____

Describe a situation in which you were able to demonstrate this skill.

1) _____

2) _____

3) _____

4) _____

5) _____

Why is this skill important to you?

1) _____

2) _____

3) _____

4) _____

5) _____

ASSESSING YOUR TOP-FIVE SKILLS

How would you like to develop or strengthen this skill?

1) _____

2) _____

3) _____

4) _____

5) _____

TRANSFERABLE SKILLS

You have chosen your five strongest and most favored skills, and you have eliminated your five least favorite skills. You are now left with a variety of skills that fall somewhere in between.

Many of these are transferable skills and it is important not to overlook or ignore them. Transferable skills are different from job-specific skills and can be utilized in almost any work setting. Examples of transferable skills include negotiating, organizing, listening, reasoning, and problem solving. These are the kinds of skills that complement job-specific skills and add that extra dimension that employers are often looking for.

Review the skills that are in the middle of your list and see which ones you would describe as transferable. Place a *T* next to them. Then as you did with your top five skills, think about a situation in which you were able to demonstrate this ability.

Knowing you have a skill and being able to comfortably talk about that skill are two very different things. Unfortunately, many people don't know how to clearly articulate their strengths or don't feel they have the right to sing their own praises. This belief places them at a distinct disadvantage when pursuing a job. Being comfortable with what you have to offer and knowing how to confidently talk about the assets you have can make the difference between being offered a job and being passed up.

Talents

Talents can be described as our natural, or innate, abilities. They are the activities we are drawn to and that we truly love doing. Each of us has our own set of talents that might include specific academic, athletic, artistic, or interpersonal abilities, as well as problem solving, reasoning, and teaching abilities.

The best way to distinguish whether an ability you have is a skill or a talent is to ask yourself the following questions:

1. What do I really love to do?

- *What are you doing when you feel completely involved and totally absorbed?*
- *What brings you joy?*

2. What do I enjoy thinking about?

- *What are the things that you find yourself pondering and ruminating?*

3. What do I enjoy learning about?

- *What kinds of things hold your attention?*
- *What do you want to learn more about?*
- *What specific areas do you not mind working hard at to expand your skills and knowledge?*

Focusing on our talents is not something that most of us spend much time doing. We either take them for granted or we downplay them because it can seem self-aggrandizing to tout something that comes naturally. But our talents are gifts to the world and it is important that we embrace them.

Take some time to think about the talents you have. You may have talents that you know you don't want to pursue. You may rediscover talents that have lain dormant for several years. Use the worksheet on the following page to list all the talents that come to mind. If you find yourself struggling with this list, ask a close friend or family member what they see as some of your talents; this might help to jump-start your thought process.

As with the skills inventory, put this exercise aside for a while and come back to it as new ideas come to you. Once you feel that you have your inventory as complete as possible, review the talents that you have listed and circle your top three. When you have your three, prioritize them in order of importance to you.

YOUR TALENTS

List your most valued talents.

_____   _____   _____

_____   _____   _____

_____   _____   _____

_____   _____   _____

_____   _____   _____

_____   _____

Your Top Three Talents

1) _____

2) _____

3) _____

You have now developed a list of five skills and three talents that are of the highest priority to you; it is important that you keep these in the forefront of you mind as you look at career possibilities. These are your strengths, assets, and unique gifts. By proactively seeking a career that will allow you to use at least some of your top skills and talents, you will greatly improve your chances of finding yourself in a rewarding and fulfilling job.

Personality Traits

The last two sections have helped you define what things you like to do and what kinds of activities come naturally to you. In this section, you are going to shift your attention from doing to being. We can spend a lot of time focusing on the skills we have to offer, but we often forget that we also have a whole set of personality traits that can also be employment assets.

Looking at the list on the following page, which words do you feel best describe you? As you review the list, be careful to not pick out words you think *should* describe you. Each of these words is an asset in its own right and none are valued higher than others. Keep in mind that employers like to have people on staff who can offer a variety of different traits. So, be honest with yourself and circle the words that fit you best.

PERSONALITY TRAITS

Circle the personality traits that describe you.

Achievement-oriented	Diligent	Open-minded
Adaptable	Easy-Going	Outgoing
Adventurous	Effective	Perceptive
Appreciative	Energetic	Persistent
Assertive	Enthusiastic	Playful
Compassionate	Flexible	Practical
Competent	Friendly	Professional
Competitive	Imaginative	Reliable
Conscientious	Independent	Resourceful
Courageous	Innovative	Responsible
Creative	Kind	Self-motivated
Decisive	Level-headed	Tactful
Dependable	Loyal	Thorough

Other _____

_____

_____

Now take another look at the personality traits that you have circled and prioritize the five that you feel best describe you. Once you have chosen your five main traits, think of a situation in which having this quality benefited you or someone else. It is easy to say that you are innovative, but it will be much more impressive and carry more weight with interviewers if you give a personal example of how being innovative has positively affected a work situation. Read through the following example.

Trait: Thorough

Situation: Jamie was part of a team that was putting together a presentation for the organization's board of directors. The program in which she worked wanted more funding to expand its services into three more schools. This was an important presentation and the team had worked very long and hard to make sure that all the facts and figures were accurate.

Jamie received a copy of the final report a day before the board meeting. Being a very thorough person, she decided to review the report one more time. She didn't expect to find any errors as the team had proofed it several times, but there on the third page was a typo that had two transposed numbers. So, instead of asking for $175,000, it looked as though they were asking for $715,000. Because of Jamie's need to be thorough, the team was spared a great deal of embarrassment.

Now use the worksheets on the following pages to go through the same exercise for your top five personality traits.

YOUR TOP FIVE PERSONALITY TRAITS

Trait #1 _____

Situation: _____

YOUR TOP FIVE PERSONALITY TRAITS

Trait #2 _____

Situation: _____

YOUR TOP FIVE PERSONALITY TRAITS, CONT'D

Trait #3 _____

Situation: _____

YOUR TOP FIVE PERSONALITY TRAITS

Trait #4 _____

Situation: _____

YOUR TOP FIVE PERSONALITY TRAITS, CONT'D

Trait #5 _____

Situation: _____

The exercises in the last two chapters have given you a lot of information about who you are and what is important to you. Before you move on to the next chapter, it might be helpful to pull together all your data and review what you have learned about yourself.

SUMMARY SHEET

Interests and Values

Top three interests:

_____

_____

_____

Top five personal values:

_____

_____

_____

_____

_____

SUMMARY SHEET, CONT'D

Top five work values:

_____

_____

_____

_____

Personality Style

Holland Inventory

Three strongest areas of interest:

_____

_____

_____

Myers-Briggs

Four preferred ways of functioning:

_____

_____

_____

_____

SUMMARY SHEET

Thoughts, Beliefs, and Motivators

Top three motivators:

_____

_____

_____

Skills, Talents, and Work Environment

Top five skills:

_____

_____

_____

_____

_____

Top three talents:

_____

_____

_____

SUMMARY SHEET, CONT'D

Top five personality traits:

_____

_____

_____

_____

_____

Now that you have a solid sense of who you are and what you have to offer, the next step is to take that information and begin exploring what kinds of work environments would best integrate and support your specific set of interests, values, skills, and personality traits.

Your Ideal Work Environment

It is easy to look at potential careers only in terms of job responsibilities and forget about the role that our work environment plays in our overall job satisfaction. Often, it's only when a problem arises that you begin to notice your environment. You may become aware of the things you don't like, and when you look for another job, you might try to make sure that those specific elements are not part of your new environment.

But that doesn't always guarantee that you'll end up in a positive and supportive environment. It just guarantees that you have eliminated those particular issues you've noticed. There simply may be a new set of other things you don't like in your new environment. Therefore, this process of elimination may not be the best way of finding a nurturing workplace.

A more effective strategy is to take time before you start looking for a job to identify what your ideal work environment would be. There are two benefits that come from doing this research. First, you will have the information you need to make intelligent and informed decisions about future jobs. Second, becoming more aware of what types of environments appeal to you may spark new ideas about what you want to be doing. For example, if you come to realize that you honestly love being outdoors, you might start thinking about how you could bring your skills to environmental work.

There are many factors to take into consideration when thinking about a work environment. Some are obvious, such as work space and geographical location, while others can be more subtle, such as the amount of contact with other people and levels of noise.

The list of questions on the following page will help you define what the ideal work environment might be like for you.

DESCRIBE YOUR IDEAL WORK ENVIRONMENT

1. Do you want to work in a specific geographical area?

   _____

   _____

2. Do you like working inside or outside? City or suburbs?

   _____

   _____

3. Do you want to work for yourself or for an organization?

   _____

   _____

4. What type of organization would you be most comfortable working for (large corporation, medium or small business, nonprofit, government)?

   _____

   _____

5. Describe your ideal office space (light, space, privacy, so on).

   _____

   _____

6. How much do you want to interact with other people on a daily basis?

   _____

   _____

DESCRIBE YOUR IDEAL WORK ENVIRONMENT

7. What types of people do you enjoy working with?

   _____

   _____

8. Are you more comfortable working as part of a team or by yourself?

   _____

   _____

9. What do you need in a supervisor to perform at your best?

   _____

   _____

10. How much structure do you need to your day? What does that structure look like?

    _____

    _____

11. How much responsibility and decision-making power do you want to have?

    _____

    _____

12. Do you want to travel for your job?

    _____

    _____

DESCRIBE YOUR IDEAL WORK ENVIRONMENT, CONT'D

13. How many hours per week are you willing to work?

   _____

   _____

14. How do you want to be recognized and rewarded at work?

   _____

   _____

15. How important is it that your core values and beliefs are congruent with those of the organization you work for (integrity, honesty, work/life balance, family, etc.)?

   _____

   _____

16. List any other characteristics that you may have thought of.

   _____

   _____

Be honest as you go through these questions. Don't censor yourself by thinking that you will never be able to get what you want, or thinking that what you want is in some way immature or irresponsible. First of all, no one will see your answers unless you want them to. And secondly, your answers will give you a great deal of useful information about what you value in your workplace. And when you know what you want, you can proactively seek it out instead of reactively bouncing from place to place hoping to find it.

There is an old adage that says you can't put a square peg in a round hole. The same can be said when discussing workers and work environments. By now, you have a good idea of what you like, what's important to you, what supports you, and what causes you to suffer. Maybe you would describe yourself as a hexagon or a decahedron. Who knows? You might even be a rhombus. Whatever your unique configuration, make sure you take the time to find the working environment that best fits your individual design.

Designing Your Dream Job

Using the information you have gathered in the previous sections, design your perfect job. Be as creative in this process as possible. Think outside the box. What is it that you would absolutely love to do? Describe as many elements of your dream job as possible and be as specific as you can. Remember, this is your ideal. There are no restrictions. You have all the skills, talents, and resources you need for any job.

You may be wondering how creating a make-believe job is going to help you find the career you want. The goal of this exercise is to help you think creatively about career possibilities. It can be very easy to limit your scope to only what you think you should do, to what you think is acceptable, or to what your logical mind is telling you is possible. Using your imagination and creativity will help you see new things and to connect the dots in different ways. You will become more aware of your transferable skills and this realization will open up all sorts of new opportunities for you.

Being free to put your dreams down on paper encourages you to think more from your heart and less from the *should* place in your mind. As a result, your ideal job will hold a great deal of information about what you truly enjoy doing and may help you realize that there are some significant changes you want to make as you head toward the right career.

For example, your ideal job may have you working for yourself, something that you have not seriously contemplated before. But as you develop this job, you begin to see that working for yourself could be a real possibility. Your thinking begins to shift and you start to look at your career from a whole new perspective.

Or maybe the job you create may not be as high powered as you thought it might be and you begin to realize that your values have changed, and that quality of life and work-life balance are more important to you now than money and prestige. You see that maybe your quest for money and prestige was coming from a place of *should*, and that has put you on the fast track to burnout. This kind of realization can be very freeing and will help ensure your ideal job is in line with your values.

There is also another reason for doing this exercise. Being able to freely create a perfect job scenario that includes all characteristics you need and want will dramatically increase your probability of finding that job, or one very similar to it. This happens more frequently than you might imagine. But it will only happen if you know what you are looking for, if you are willing to go after it, and if you believe in your ability to achieve it.

Contrary to popular belief, there is nothing wrong with going for your dreams. If you fall short, you will still end up far ahead of where you would have been had you not tried at all. This is your life and you've got one shot at it. Why not make it the best it can be?

Use the worksheets on the following pages to describe your dream job.

WHAT IS YOUR DREAM JOB?

What industry are you working in?

_____

What position do you have?

_____

What are your job responsibilities?

_____

_____

_____

What does your work environment look like?

_____

_____

_____

What kinds of people are you working with?

_____

_____

_____

WHAT IS YOUR DREAM JOB?

How much money are you making?
___

How many hours a week do you work?
___

What kind of boss do you have?
___
___
___

What's the best thing about this job?
___
___
___

Hopefully, this exercise has helped you generate some new ideas about career possibilities, as well as helped you think about your old ideas from a broad perspective. Maybe you have discovered a brand new career idea that you want to pursue, or maybe you have several ideas that you want to check out. It is now time for you to take action and start moving toward your new career.

FINDING THE RIGHT CAREER PATH

Exploring Your Career Landscape

Assessing Your Options

Places to Look

People to Know

Gathering Your Data

Now it is time for the exploration and research phase of your career development process. What are the careers that you want to learn more about? As you compile your list of potential careers, don't be afraid to let your imagination run free. Is there a career that has always interested you, but that you've dismissed because it doesn't fall into the "normal and sensible" category? Is there a career that came up as you worked through the self-discovery exercises that you had never thought about before? If so, put them both on your list.

> **Your life will be no better than the plans you make and the actions you take. You are the architect and builder of your own life, fortune, and destiny.**
> **-Alfred Montapert.**

Remember, at this point you are just gathering information. You don't have to make any commitments. And who knows what you'll learn from the information you get? Maybe you'll find out that one of the careers that interested you is actually very boring. Or maybe you'll find that one of them is just perfect for you. At this point, you want to explore any career that holds interest for you and gather as much data about each of them as you can. You will have time to analyze and evaluate your information later, before making decisions.

But what if you still don't know what careers you want to explore? If you find yourself struggling to come up with some potential career paths, there are several steps you can take. The first would be to ask your family and close friends what careers they see as a good fit for you. Notice any overlaps in their responses. If there are two are three careers that come up repeatedly, start researching those.

Secondly, go back over the information you have gathered about yourself from the "Getting to Know You" and "Getting to Know the Professional You" chapters. Read through the data as if it belonged to someone else. Taking a more objective stance will help you see commonalities and themes and might make it easier for you to come up with a few career possibilities. And finally, if those two steps don't elicit anything, just choose a career and start the exploration process. Just doing the research on one career might help jumpstart thoughts and ideas on other careers that interest you.

Assessing Your Options

Although exploring different career options can be very exciting, it can also be somewhat daunting. There is a great deal of information out there and it's easy to become overwhelmed by it all if you don't have a structured plan of action.

The best way to start this process is to choose one career and then write down all the information you want to gather on that particular career. What are your questions? What do you want to know? Then go back through your list and next to each piece of information or question you have written down, write down the resource or referral where you can get that piece of data. Use the resources listed in this book to help you.

Let's say you have some interest in becoming a physical therapist. Here are some questions you might ask, and next to each question is a resource where you could find the answer.

1. What degree or special training do I need?	Internet sites on physical therapy careers.
2. How much does one earn in this field?	*The American Almanac of Jobs and Salaries*
3. What is the demand for physical therapists?	*Occupational Outlook Handbook*
4. What types of people are most successful in this field?	Informational interview
5. What are the positive/negative aspects of this profession?	Volunteer/internship

Clarifying the information you need before you start will help you stay focused and on track. At the end of each research session, review your list and see if there are other questions or issues that have surfaced. This will help to keep the process manageable and moving forward.

If you're not sure where to find something, leave it blank. As you get more familiar with the resources available, you will be able to fill in the blanks. Start with the first piece of information for which you have a resource and then continue the process until you have collected all the data you need on that particular job or industry. Then move to the next career idea.

There are three main sources of information you can access as you start your career exploration. You are one source. You are the only one who will be able to answer questions such as How much money do I want to make? and Does this job fit well with my skills and interests? These are the kinds of questions that you will eventually spend time answering as you evaluate each career.

For the rest of the information you require, you will need to turn to external resources. These resources can be divided into two categories: places and people.

Places to Look

For finding up-to-date facts or basic information about a career such as degree requirements, salary, or potential growth in a certain field, you can use the resources found in the library, on the Internet, or in trade publications. These resources can give you the latest research and information on all careers and will provide a good starting place for you and your initial inquiries.

USING YOUR LIBRARY

Your local library contains numerous resources and reference guides that you can use to find the answers to many of your career questions. The following resources can be very helpful in providing you with relevant career information.

Dictionary of Occupational Titles (DOT)

This reference guide lists more than 25,000 jobs and provides comprehensive descriptions of job duties and the skill level involved in each.

The Guide for Occupational Exploration (GOE)

This book expands on the information found in the *DOT* and lets you explore a variety of occupations that require the use of similar skills. One of its most useful features is the question-answer format that suggest inquiries such as What kind of work would I do? or What skills are needed?

The Occupational Outlook Handbook (OOH)

This book is published biennially. It provides general information about what people in each field do and what they earn. It also describes the types of education and training each field requires, and the current demand there. It profiles more than 300 occupations and thousands of jobs within those occupations.

The American Almanac of Jobs and Salaries

This almanac is published biennially in June and provides job descriptions and pay rates for hundreds of occupations.

USING THE INTERNET

The Internet is another invaluable resource, but because of the immense amount of information that is available online, it is very important to have a clear idea of exactly what information you are trying to get so that you don't spend unnecessary hours surfing from site to site. All three of the government guides mentioned above are available online. Another valuable tool is O*NET Online, (online.onetcenter.org), which is the online version of the *Dictionary of Occupational Titles*. Clicking "Skills Search" will allow you to use your list of skills to find matching occupations.

The Internet is also a good resource for finding specific information regarding training, degrees, salaries, job outlook, and growth potential of different occupations. By entering phrases—"architecture career", for instance—into a search engine, you will be able to bring up the latest information about that career. Make sure you check the source and date of the information given to ensure that it is accurate. For more Internet resources see the "For Your Reference" chapter at the end of this book.

People to Know

The other external source of information is people. People have a wealth of knowledge to share if you are willing to ask. Your friends, family, and professional colleagues are a good starting place. Talk to them about your ideas. Ask them questions and bounce ideas off of them. They will give you names of people to talk with. As you talk with these new people, they will also know people. Doors will open and opportunities will arise. This is person-to-person networking, and it is one of the best ways of collecting career information.

INFORMATIONAL INTERVIEWS

The ultimate person-to-person networking tool is the informational interview. An informational interview involves talking with people who are currently working in a particular field to gain a better understanding of an occupation or industry.

Informational interviews provide an opportunity to ask all the questions you have about a specific industry, to get a close look at the work environment, and to gain a good sense of whether or not you would fit into this type of work setting. They also can give you the perfect opportunity to practice your interview skills in a less stressful environment, thus building your confidence for future job interviews.

But one of the best things about doing informational interviews is that you gain visibility. You are demonstrating your skills, interests, and talents in the questions you ask and the way you engage in the conversation. You are talking with a potential employer and through your conversation they will gain a sense of who you are and what you could bring to the workplace. Even if they don't have an appropriate opening in their office, they may know of other jobs that would be a good fit for you, and refer you to other people to talk with. More doors will open and more opportunities will present themselves.

To get the most out of an informational interview, it is important to think carefully about what you want to ask, and to write your questions before you go to the meeting. Remember, the purpose of this meeting is twofold. The first is to gather information about this industry. The second is to leave a positive impression on the person you are talking with. And one way to do that is to make sure that you are asking interesting and engaging questions.

There are several ways to address an issue, and depending on the question you choose to ask, you will get different responses. So, it is important to be very clear on what it is you want to learn about a job or industry and then ask the questions that will elicit such information.

Let's say you are thinking about becoming a pharmacist. You set up a meeting with your local pharmacist to learn more about what she does. Here are two types of questions you might ask.

Closed Questions:

1. Do you like your job?

2. How long have you been a pharmacist?

3. How many hours do you work per week?

4. What kind of degree or licensing do you need to become a pharmacist?

Open-Ended Questions:

1. What do you like about being a pharmacist?

2. What are some of the downsides to being a pharmacist?

3. Tell me about the process of getting licensed?

4. What kind of person do you think makes a good pharmacist?

5. How do you deal with difficult customers?

Clearly, the second set of questions will elicit more information than the first. They are softer and are more likely to initiate a conversation that might lead to other questions and information you might not have thought about. Open-ended questions show that you have put some real time, energy, and thought into what kind of information you want to obtain, which will leave a positive impression of you with the person you interviewed.

It can be intimidating to set up your first informational interview, especially if you don't have a name of a specific person at the company. However, if you call the company and explain why you are calling and what you are looking for, most receptionists will know whom to refer you to. If they don't, ask for someone in the human resources department.

The good news is that most people love to talk about their job and their organization, and will be more than willing to sit down with you to answer your questions. And once you have your first interview under your belt, the rest will be a breeze.

As you prepare for your interview, try to use as many open-ended, conversational questions as possible. Make sure your list of questions is not too long, but that it captures the essential information you want. Here are some examples of questions you might ask:

- What are the duties and responsibilities of your job?
- What do you find most satisfying and most frustrating about your job?
- What was your training and background coming into this field?
- What is a typical day like for you?
- How would you describe your work environment?
- What kinds of interaction do you have with peers, colleagues, supervisors, etc?
- What are the opportunities for growth?
- What is the best way to get into this field?
- What kind of support is available?

- What sort of compensation can one expect?
- What kinds of people experience the greatest success in this field?
- Do you feel your work is meaningful and important?
- If you were ever to leave this job, what would be the reason?

Your questions will differ depending on who you are talking with and what you want to learn. One interview may be for collecting factual data, while the next may be to understand the subtleties of a particular workplace or occupation. As you conduct more of these interviews, you will become skilled and comfortable at preparing and asking questions.

For a more thorough discussion of informational interviews and other networking techniques, don't miss the WetFeet Insider Guide *Networking Works!*, available at www.WetFeet.com.

VOLUNTEERING

Volunteering is a great way to explore career options. Volunteering gives you the chance to see first-hand how things really work in an organization and experience the ups and downs that come with that particular field. You are able to see if your temperament, skills, and values are congruent with certain environments without having to commit to a long-term job.

Volunteering helps you develop a network of contacts in your field, and will allow you to get the inside information on upcoming employment opportunities. It also gives you work experience in the field that interests you, which can be a big plus on your resume.

To get the most from volunteering, it is important to be very clear on why you are volunteering and what you want to get from the experience. Is there a specific skill you want to learn or develop? Is there a certain environment or population you want experience working with?

Maybe you are interested in teaching, but want to work in a school setting first to see what it's really like interacting with students of a particular age. Maybe you are interested in health care, but want to experience working with different specialists before you decide exactly which area you want to pursue. So you might decide to volunteer in a hospital or neighborhood clinic. Or maybe you are thinking about a legal career. Volunteering in a community law office will give you the experience you need to help you figure out if law is the right avenue for you.

There are many places you can get information about volunteer opportunities in your community. Most communities have volunteer centers listed in the phone book. Your local United Way office is an excellent resource for up-to-date information on all the agencies it supports in your area. Contact your local Chamber of Commerce for a list of local nonprofits that are looking for volunteer assistance. And most public libraries, as well as college and university libraries and career centers, provide volunteer information.

If you're confused about which career might fit you best, if you are struggling to choose between several careers, or if you just don't know what career path to pursue, volunteering may be the best way to get your questions answered. Volunteering takes the hypothetical and makes it real. Gaining a bit of direct exposure to a field will make it much easier to determine whether or not you want to pursue a career in that field.

INTERNSHIPS

Another good way of trying out a potential career is to do an internship. An internship offers you the opportunity to gain experience in a field that interests you. People often think that internships are only for students, but anyone in the process of changing careers or thinking about different career options can also benefit from an internship.

An internship offers you a relatively risk-free way of exploring a potential career, as well as a good way to gain work experience and develop job skills. It also provides you with opportunities for networking and can significantly increase your chances of securing a rewarding full-time position.

Internships can be paid or not, full- or part-time and they are available in just about every field. If you are still in school, you have access to information about possible internships thorough your Career Center. If you are no longer in school, you will need to begin networking with family, friends, and colleagues. You could also contact your college alumni association to see how they might help you. And don't leave without visiting company websites and internship websites.

There is a great deal of information available about how to find, apply, and get the most out of an internship. To get the most out of this information spend some time up front clarifying as best you can exactly what it is you are looking for. You are much more likely to land the internship you want if you can clearly articulate what that internship looks like.

For a full discussion of internships and finding or creating the right one for you, check out the WetFeet Insider Guide *Getting Your Ideal Internship*, available at www.WetFeet.com.

Gathering Your Data

You are going to be collecting a great deal of information throughout this process and it's important to have some way of keeping track of it so that you can access it when you need it. One way to organize your data is to keep it in a notebook, giving each career its own section. That way you would have a specific place to put your notes, interview questions and answers, names of contact people, and your thoughts and impressions about each career. It might also be useful to develop worksheets for different activities so that you have a uniform way of gathering your information. Following are some examples of possible worksheets.

FACTS AND FIGURES

Career/Job_____

This worksheet can be used to collect hard data from books, the Internet, trade publications, and so on. These may include answers to questions such as:

1. What kind of degree/training is needed?

2. What is the current salary range?

3. How many hours a week can I expect to work?

4. How much demand is there for people in this field?

5. What kinds of skills/talents/knowledge are needed?

6. _____

7. _____

8. _____

Other information I need to get:

_____

_____

_____

_____

INFORMATIONAL INTERVIEWS

Before the Interview:

Company Name_____

Address_____

Person to Interview_____

Date/Time of Interview_____

What information do I want to make sure I get?

_____

_____

_____

_____

What questions do I need to ask? (Make them open-ended.)

_____

_____

_____

_____

_____

FINDING THE RIGHT CAREER PATH

EXPLORING YOUR CAREER LANDSCAPE

INFORMATIONAL INTERVIEWS

After the Interview:

What were my overall impressions?

_____

_____

What were the positive aspects of this job?

_____

_____

What were the negative aspects?

_____

_____

What other information do I need?

_____

_____

Every person has her own way of organizing information, so use whatever method works best for you. As you collect your information, try to utilize as many different resources as possible. Talk with friends and colleagues. Schedule informational interviews. Do research on the Internet. You want to get as accurate a picture as possible of each career, as this will make your evaluation and decision-making much easier.

FINDING THE RIGHT CAREER PATH

Evaluation and Decision-Making

Mapping Your Options

Charting Your Path

EVALUATION AND DECISION-MAKING

Now that you have collected the information your need about yourself and potential careers paths, the next step is to pull this data together and create a coherent picture of the career possibilities that most interest you. This can be difficult because this is the point in the process where you are most likely to encounter the fears, resistance, and critical voices that arise with any life change. But in order to move forward, you must be willing to tolerate the doubts, ambiguity, and anxiety that are inherent in the process of change.

> **Once you make a decision, the universe conspires to make it happen.**
> **-Ralph Waldo Emerson**

This chapter will give you the tools and strategies to effectively synthesize and evaluate the internal (self-knowledge) and the external (career data) information that you have collected. This chapter will also discuss the decision-making process and the different ways people make decisions. Becoming more familiar with your individual decision-making style will allow you to be more comfortable and empowered as you decide which career(s) you would like to pursue.

Mapping Your Options

Information is only useful if it helps you make choices that move your life forward in a positive and rewarding way. Right now you have a lot of information on different pieces of paper. In this state, it's fairly useless. It will only be beneficial to you if you are able to evaluate it in the context of your goal, which is to find a career that fits your skills, values, and interests. The exercises on the following pages are designed to help you synthesize the data you have collected and evaluate it in terms of what you are looking for in a career.

It may be tempting to skip this part. Maybe you feel that you know what career you want to pursue. Maybe you are feeling some resistance to taking the time and energy to work through these exercises. Or maybe you are still feeling confused about all this career stuff and just want to take the fast track to your next job. Whatever your resistance, try to put it aside and focus your attention on completing the exercises.

You have done a lot of work to collect your data and now you need to take the time to carefully evaluate it. This is the crux of the career development process: integrating all the pieces into a cohesive plan that fits with who you are and what you need in order to have a challenging and satisfying career. This is where the creative intersects with the practical, and where possibilities, opportunities, and dreams all come together to form your ideal career.

IDEAL JOB VS REALITY

This exercise will help you compare the careers you have researched to what you feel to be the ideal job for you.

Divide a piece of paper into two columns. On the left-hand side, list all the components of the ideal job you created in the "Getting to Know the Professional You" chapter. These would include things such as position, job responsibilities, salary, specifics about work environment, motivators, kinds of people you'd work with, autonomy, work hours, etc. On the right-hand side of the page, rate each item one through five, with one being the least important and five being the most important. Add up all the points and write the total at the bottom of the right column.

Using one form for each career researched, rate how well it meets the criteria you've set for your perfect job. Label each sheet with the career you are evaluating to keep track of the information.

Since you're assessing careers against your ideal, it is likely that most of the careers that you research will fall short of rating all fives. But that is okay. This exercise will help you get a clearer picture of how actual jobs compare with what you really want. It is not likely that one career will have everything that you want; but hopefully, each will have enough to let you see that many of the components you want in a job are possible to have.

This exercise will also allow you to see if there are certain fields and career types that offer more of what you are looking for than others.

SKILLS, INTERESTS, AND VALUES

This exercise is similar to the previous exercise, but this time you are evaluating how well each career matches, or gives you the opportunity to use, your priority skills, interests, and values.

Divide a sheet of paper into two columns. Taking the information you gathered in the "Getting to Know You" and "Getting to Know the Professional You" chapters, list your top-three interests, your top-five professional skills, your top-five personal skills, and your top-five business values in the left-hand column. On the right-hand side of the page, rate each item one through five, with one being the least important and five being the most important.

Once again, using one form per career, evaluate each on how well it matches your top skills, interests, and values. Rate each item honestly, and then total your points at the bottom. This evaluation process will only be useful if you are as objective as possible in your rating.

Objectively rating each career in the areas that are most important to you will give you a very good sense of which careers are most compatible with what you want and need. It will also help you to see whether or not you have all the information you need about each career.

EVALUATION AND DECISION-MAKING

Deciding on a career path is not a purely intellectual process. Your final decision will most likely be based on input from both your mind and your heart. But it can be easy to get pulled off track along the way by your own emotions and well-meaning friends and family who may or may not understand why you are looking at certain kinds of careers. Therefore, it can be very helpful to have some concrete, objective data that you can turn to when you feel yourself losing focus.

As you review the results of the last two exercises, you may find that you have narrowed your focus down to two or three careers that truly interest you. The problem now is making the decision as to which one you want to pursue at this time. Even if you find there is only one career that interests you, you still have to decide whether or not this is the best career for you at this time. The following section will help you make that decision.

Picking and Choosing

Making decisions is a fundamental life skill. Whether we like it or not, we are constantly making decisions. Oftentimes, we think that we can defer the process by not making any decision at all. But, even in our decision not to decide, we have made a decision!

So, given that making decisions is an integral part our lives, it is important to be comfortable with our decision-making technique. There is no one way to make decisions. Each of us has our own unique style. The key, however, is to be very aware of what our style is so that we can begin to recognize those patterns of behavior that are helpful and those that create stumbling blocks.

How do you make decisions? Are you someone who makes decisions quickly, or are you more methodical? Do you need to gather lots of information, or are you satisfied with a smaller set of relevant facts? Do you seek input from other people, or do you prefer to figure things out on your own? Are you swayed more by facts or by intuition?

Decision-making is not an exact science. The outcome is not guaranteed no matter how carefully you think about your decision—and therein lies the rub. You will always be presented with more than one choice. How will you know which choice is the right one for you?

Some people deal with these feelings of uncertainty by making decisions quickly and ignoring or denying the emotional aspect of their decisions. Others find themselves frozen by the weight of their decision and the impact it could have on all involved. Neither of these methods is particularly effective.

If you find yourself in this situation as you are thinking about career choices, the following questions may help jumpstart the decision-making process and get you moving forward again.

EVALUATION AND DECISION-MAKING

1. What is the actual decision I need to make? What is the core issue? What is the objective of this decision?

2. Can I break this decision down into smaller parts? Is there more than one issue involved? How can I separate them so that I have a more clear picture of my goal?

3. How many people and how much information do I really need to make this decision? (Too much input can be as detrimental as too little.)

4. What is my gut telling me? (Once you get all the information you need, it may be useful to sit calmly by yourself and listen to what your body and heart are telling you.)

5. Where can I get the support I need when I am feeling stuck, scared, or unsure of how to proceed? (Make sure that you have one or two people who will be willing to listen and ask the kinds of questions that help you clarify your decision.)

Once you make your decision, go with it. Try not to second-guess yourself. Be confident in your choice knowing that you were thoughtful and thorough in the process. Don't listen to the voices of doubt that will most likely pop up. Instead, focus your energy and attention on reaching and successfully implementing your decision.

Remember that decision-making is a process. Although the content will be different with each decision, your basic process of coming to a decision will stay pretty much the same. That is why it is important to know what your process is and where it might not be working as well as it could. Having a solid and consistent process in place will enable you to make decisions with more ease, confidence, and success.

This last exercise is designed to help you come to a decision about which career(s) you want to pursue by integrating what you have learned through your personal reactions to the objective data. Take each career that interests you and answer the questions below. Think about what is most important to you in a job. What issues carry the most weight? There may be an issue that is not listed in the next exercise. Feel free to add it to the list of questions.

FINDING THE RIGHT CAREER PATH

EVALUATION AND DECISION-MAKING

As you go through the following exercise, listen carefully to what your heart and gut are telling you. They usually will point you in the right direction.

DECISION-MAKING CHECKLIST

Career Field _____

Specific Job (if known) _____

Mark each question with a Y (yes), N (no), or NS (not sure).

1a. Do you possess the skills necessary to work in this field? _____

1b. If not, are you willing to put in the time, energy, and money to gain these skills? _____

2. Would you be working with people who can challenge and support you? _____

3. Are you comfortable with the benefits package offered? _____

4. Would this job allow you to maximize your talents and your potential? _____

5. Does the work environment feel comfortable? _____

6. Would this career or job allow for professional growth and development? _____

7. Is this job congruent with your personal values and mission? _____

8. Are you comfortable with the sacrifices that you would have to make, such as having to work long hours, enduring high stress, or traveling? _____

9. Do you feel excited, energized, and enthusiastic when you envision yourself in this career? _____

10. Given everything you know at this time, do you feel that this is the right career for you? _____

EVALUATION AND DECISION-MAKING

Up to this point, the focus of your process has been to narrow down the number of career ideas you have, so that you can find the one that truly fits this point in your professional life. Now that you have accomplished that, it is time to take the next step, which is committing to your path and launching an employment search that will successfully end with you being hired into your ideal job.

Getting Started

Developing an Action Plan

Preparing for Your Job Campaign

Starting Your Search

Overcoming Common Obstacles

Focus and Motivation

You are now ready to take the next step by launching your job campaign. This chapter will give you the tools and strategies to pursue the job(s) you've targeted.

Before you get started with the actual to-dos of the job campaign, it is important to take some time to assess your level of personal commitment to this job search. Are you excited about the job you have chosen? Can you envision yourself in that position? Are you motivated to do the work necessary to make your dream a reality? Are you truly committed to this leg of the journey?

Only you will know the answers to these questions. Be honest with yourself. How committed are you? How badly do you want this? If you find that this job, or this process, doesn't hold enough energy for you at this point in time, you might want to review your self-assessment and research sections for other options.

Maybe you have made your decision according to someone else's criteria. Maybe you are trying to get enthusiastic about something that really isn't a good fit for you. You are the one who is going to be employed in this position—make sure that it is something that truly energizes and excites you.

However, if you know deep down in your heart that this is the right job to pursue, and if you are ready and willing to devote the time and energy needed to see this job campaign through to the end, then let's get started.

Developing an Action Plan

One of the best ways to keep motivated and ensure success during this phase of your career development journey is to develop a detailed action plan. This plan needs to address the following questions:

- What is your goal?
- What steps do you have to take to reach your goal?
- What is your timeline?

DEFINING YOUR GOAL

The first step to any action plan is stating the intended outcome. In this case, your intended outcome most likely is securing the job that you chose in the last chapter. It is very important to be as specific as possible when you are developing your outcome statement.

There are three reasons for this. The first, and most practical, is that it is much easier to build a more effective action plan around a clear and solid outcome. The second reason is that the more clear you are about what you are looking for, the easier it is for people to give you relevant and useful referrals. And the last reason is that we draw our intentions into our lives. Therefore, if you know exactly what it is that you want, there is a great likelihood that you will get it.

Notice the difference between the two goal statements in the examples following.

A. To secure a position as a paralegal in a downtown law firm

B. To secure a position as a paralegal in a small local law firm that specializes in environmental law

A. To secure a position as an advertising sales representative in a small, but successful advertising firm

B. To secure a position as an advertising sales representative working for one of the following sports magazines: *Skiing*, *Adventure Sports*, *Windsurfing*, or *Mountain Bike Action*

The more specific the outcome, the easier it will be to outline the action steps necessary to reach that outcome. Take time to carefully think about not only the position you want, but also the type of environment, the mission, and the values you want the company to embrace. If you know the names of specific organizations you want to work for be sure to include them in your goal statement. That will help to keep your action steps more focused.

STEPS TO REACH YOUR GOAL

One of the easiest ways to get sidetracked in your job search is to become overwhelmed with the enormity of the process. The endpoint can often seem a long way from your starting point. One way to lessen this perceived gap is to take your desired goal and break it down into smaller, more workable pieces. As you complete each of these smaller tasks, your sense of accomplishment will keep you motivated and moving toward the realization of your goal.

It sometimes can be tricky to break your overall goal into small enough steps. You might be tempted to try to skip over steps or combine two or three together because you want to hurry up and get to your goal. This approach does not work well. It will really be to your benefit in the long run to take your time and carefully plan out all the things you need to do to reach your goal.

Some obvious things that will need to be done are to create a resume and cover letter. Others to-dos may include setting up appointments with specific networking contacts, contacting organizations, distributing your resume on certain Internet employment sites, and contacting your college placement office.

Your to-do list will depend on the type of campaign strategy you decide to employ. The more proactive the strategy, the more action steps you will have to complete. If you choose to take a wait-and-see approach there won't be as much for you to do, but you lower your chances of reaching your goal. There will be more information about different job campaign strategies in the next section.

For a complete discussion of resumes and cover letters, check out the WetFeet Insider Guide *Killer Cover Letters and Resumes*, available at www.WetFeet.com.

PLANNING YOUR TIMELINE

To ensure that you stay on track and keep moving forward toward your goal, it is important to create a timeline that you can stick to. It is one thing to have all these wonderful action steps in place, but if you don't have any defined timeline in which to accomplish these tasks, you could be working on this project for a very long time.

The first question is what you think is a reasonable amount of time to set aside for achieving your overall goal. This answer will vary depending on what your specific goal is and how big the gap is between that goal and where you are right now. For example, if your goal is to become a financial advisor, there are tests you must pass before you can start working. You will have to factor when these tests are given and how long you will need to study for them and what happens if you don't pass them on the first go-around. In this case, there is a large time lapse between the start and finish.

On the other hand, if your goal is to be hired as a graphic designer, and you have your portfolio ready to go and know what companies you want to approach, the gap you have to bridge is not as wide. The size of the gap is neither a good or bad thing. It is just something that needs to be recognized and taken into consideration when developing your timeline.

Another point to consider when creating your timeline is your personal working style. Are you someone who is highly action-oriented and works best under a little pressure?

Or do you prefer taking your time with things? The key here is to find the pace that will keep you moving forward without putting too much pressure on you but also without being so lax that you lose your interest and focus. Only you know what the right pace will be for you.

Once you have decided on your overall timeline, the next step is to create a schedule for completing the smaller action steps. One of the most effective ways to ensure that you continue to accomplish these smaller tasks is to work from a weekly schedule.

List all the tasks you have to do to reach your goal, organize them into similar groups, such as networking, resume writing, and researching companies, and prioritize them based on what makes sense to do first, second, third, and so on.

Once you have a sense of the order of your tasks, create a weekly schedule to make sure you achieve these tasks. Choose two or three items from your list to accomplish each week. It can be tempting to take on a lot in the beginning of this process. You are feeling energized and motivated and want to reach your goal as quickly as possible. But it is more effective to start with a lower number of items the first few weeks so that you will have a higher likelihood of completing them.

Unfortunately, life often does get in the way of good intentions and you might find that you can't finish all the things you set out to do. This may leave you feeling discouraged and can kill your momentum. By keeping your list short, you are much more likely to experience success, and being successful will give you the confidence to keep moving toward your goal.

Once you have decided on your items for the week, schedule specific times on your calendar to work on them. If you are going to call someone to set up a meeting, write the call in your appointment book. If you need to do research, block off some time for that. If possible, choose times that are not sandwiched between other activities. Give yourself the time and space you need to really focus on the task at hand.

Set a specific time each week to review what you have accomplished and set your schedule for the coming week. Once you have it completed, post it where you will see it often. (There is a great deal of validity to the saying, "Out of sight, out of mind.") Therefore, do whatever it takes to remind you to take action. Write the schedule in color and post it on your bulletin board, mirror, or wall. Put it on your computer calendar. Tell your friends and family what you are working on and ask them to give you gentle reminders.

Weeks can go by quickly and unless you stay on track, it can be very easy to let things slide. Once that starts to happen, it can be difficult to get yourself up and running again. But if you can keep moving forward at a steady pace, you'll be surprised at how quickly you can reach your goal.

Preparing for Your Job Campaign

Before you actually start your job search, you want to make sure that you have a great resume and cover letter ready to go, and that you are comfortable with your interview skills. This section is going to briefly discuss each of these. For in-depth information on each of these areas, please see the list of WetFeet Insider Guides in the back of the book.

RESUMES

The purpose of a resume is to communicate your qualifications for a specific job position to prospective employers. Thus, your resume should highlight the unique blend of skills, experience, strengths, and accomplishments that make you a serious contender for a job. Getting hired is a competition and being able to design a resume that best conveys your abilities will give you an edge over other competitors.

There are three different styles of resumes, chronological, functional, and combination style. The chronological resume focuses primarily on your work experience, listing the positions you have held in reverse order with the most recent one first. This style of resume is good to use when you are applying for a position in a field where you have had a great deal of experience because it allows you to highlight your relevant work experience. However, it is not as effective in situations where you do not have much work experience in that particular area.

The second type is the functional resume. This resume highlights your skills and abilities rather than the specific work situations in which you have obtained these skills. The functional resume is good to use if you are trying to enter a field in which you don't have a lot of experience.

The third type of resume integrates elements of the previous two styles. This can be a more difficult resume to write as it contains both a brief employment history with job titles and work dates, as well as highlights your skills and competencies.

What resume you choose will depend on your particular situation. But there are some general tips to keep in mind no matter which resume you use:

- Your resume should clearly state your professional objective.

- Your resume should clearly communicate your major strengths—not just your accomplishments.

- Resumes should be no longer than two pages, unless otherwise specified.

- Resumes should not include references; they can be supplied at your interview.

- Your resume should be attractive to the eye; use good weight paper of conservative color, make sure there is plenty of white space, and avoid fancy fonts.

Employers spend about one minute per resume so you want to make sure that yours will stand out. It needs to be appealing to the eye, in a logical format that is easy to read, and it needs to capture your strengths in clear, concise language. If you are not super confident with your writing or design skill, you might consider working with a professional resume writer who could help you create a stand-out resume.

COVER LETTERS

Your resume always needs to be accompanied by a cover letter. The purpose of the cover letter is to convince the employer to review your resume and invite you for an interview. The cover letter needn't be long, but it should grab the attention of the reader and direct her focus to what you want her to notice most about your qualifications.

In general, a cover letter consists of four paragraphs. The first paragraph addresses why you are writing to this employer. You might start off with a statement such as, "I am writing in response to the ad you placed in the *Omaha Sun* on Sunday, November 23, 2005 for the position of financial assistant."

The second paragraph explains why you are interested in this job and want to work for this employer. It might read something like, "I have just completed an internship with Stevens and Associates and am very interested in an opportunity to work with you and your staff at The Northrup Group."

The third paragraph outlines your specific qualifications for this particular job. This should be relatively short as they have your resume, but you want to make sure that you highlight what you think will make you stand out from other candidates.

The last paragraph states what you hope will happen next. You might close your letter by saying, "I would welcome the chance to speak with you personally to learn more about the position and answer any questions you may have. I will follow up with you in a week to answer any preliminary questions. Thank you for your time and consideration."

If possible, keep cover letters to one page. Remember, employers are busy people and they don't have time to read long, drawn out letters. You want to capture the essence of yourself in a brief, articulate, and energetic letter. Here are some generic tips to remember as you create your cover letter.

- Cover letters should include your contact information: phone number, address, and email
- Include the date above the inside address
- Cover letters should be addressed to a specific person
- Avoid using abbreviations and acronyms
- The letter should be typed, not handwritten; avoid fancy fonts
- Make sure you proofread the letter several times; sending a letter with typos will not leave a positive impression
- Be sure to always include a *thank you* in the close of your letter

For a full discussion on how to write perfect cover letters and resumes, see the WetFeet Insider Guide *Killer Cover Letters and Resumes*, available at www.WetFeet.com.

INTERVIEWING

Although your first interview may be a while down the road, it is never too early to start practicing your interview skills. Going through a job interview can be an intimidating experience, but your fear and anxiety can be greatly reduced if you take the time to prepare before you get to your first interview.

One way to prepare is to think about the questions you might be asked and write out answers to each one. Although this may seem like a large task, all possible interview questions can be broken down into four categories.

Open-Ended Questions

These are questions such as "Tell me about yourself," or "Tell me about your long-range career goals." These kinds of questions are designed to see how well you can formulate an idea and carry it through to its conclusion without getting sidetracked or losing your train of thought.

Negative Bait

These questions are designed to see how you would describe a negative situation in your last job. You might be asked, "What is the worst job you ever had and why," or "Tell me about the worst supervisor you've had." In asking these questions, employers are looking to see how you relate to less than ideal situations. Will you come across as negative and petty or mature and understanding?

Specific Work Questions

This is where you will need to be able to clearly talk about not only what skills you have, but be able to give specific examples of how you have used these skills in your previous jobs. It might be useful to go back and review the exercises in "Getting to Know the Professional You."

Who You Are

Employers like to get a sense of who you are beyond the nervous interview candidate so they often will ask you questions about what you enjoy doing outside of work and what kinds of interests and hobbies you have.

Although there may always be a surprise question or two in an interview, the majority of the questions can be anticipated, therefore making it possible to practice beforehand. Taking the time to think about and rehearse your answers will allow you to go into the interview session knowing that you have a solid arsenal of responses at your disposal.

One of the best ways to practice is to role-play with a friend. Having to actually respond to questions in front of someone is a much more authentic way of previewing the interview than just going over the answers in your head.

This kind of preparation will help alleviate much of the initial stress and anxiety of the interview experience. And when you are less stressed, you can think and speak more clearly, thus coming across as a well-prepared, professional applicant.

Here are some other steps you can take to ensure that you have a positive interview experience:

- Arrive early enough to be able to get settled and relax
- Dress appropriately; consider the image you want to convey
- Don't chew gum or drink beverages
- Have a list of relevant questions prepared for the interviewer
- Listen carefully to each question and make sure you understand it before you answer
- Speak clearly and confidently; try not to use too many slang phrases
- Be honest and be yourself
- Follow up the interview with a thank-you note to your interviewer

Knowing Your Rights

There are clear state and federal guidelines for the kinds of questions employers are allowed to ask individuals during the interview process, and it is expected that employers adhere to these guidelines. However, despite the laws prohibiting certain kinds of questions, you may find that some employers continue to include illegal questions in their interviews. Illegal questions probe the areas of your life that are related to your race, religion, sex, national origin, disability, or age.

It is important for you to know what these laws are and how they could affect you so that you can be properly prepared in case you are asked an inappropriate question. For more information about employment discrimination, visit the Equal Employment Opportunity Commission's web site at www.eeoc.gov.

Learn more about perfecting your interview skills with the WetFeet Insider Guide *Ace Your Interview!*, available at www.WetFeet.com.

Starting Your Search

Now that you have completed your preparation work, it is time to begin your job-search campaign. You can employ two basic categories when searching for a job. First, there is the one-dimensional reactive approach, in which you send out many resumes to job announcements in the paper and on the Internet and then wait for someone to call you and ask you in for an interview.

Although newspapers and the Internet are all viable resources in a job campaign, they only can offer you a small percentage of the available job openings. This is because 80 percent of potential jobs are what are known as *hidden jobs*. These are the jobs that can only be accessed through direct person-to-person contact, such as networking and informational interviewing. The remaining 20 percent of the jobs are those you see advertised.

So, it probably makes more sense to employ a multidimensional approach to your job search using a variety of search techniques, focusing a major part of your energy on networking. By being more proactive and searching out the connections that can help you reach the people in charge of hiring, you will have a much greater chance of landing the specific job you want.

Landing a job is a little like fishing. You want to have as many lines in the water as possible and you want to spend most of your time in the areas that have the most fish. You can never be sure where a potential job might come from, so availing yourself of as many different resources as possible is important. The secret is to always be doing something that will increase your chances of being hired. People who wait for the phone to ring may have to wait for a long time.

One effective strategy might be to divide your time among the following activities, prioritizing each one based on the order in which it is listed.

NETWORKING

Networking is by far the most productive use of your search time. But to get the most from your networking, you need to be very clear about exactly what it is you are looking for. What kind of position do you want? What kind of a company do you want to work for? What skills and knowledge can you bring to this job?

When you are talking with people about your job search, be careful not to assume that they know what you want. Clearly articulate that you are actively looking for a job. Be specific in why or how someone might be able to help you. This person might work in the field that you are interested in. Or maybe you know he has a connection to a company at which you would like to work. Make sure that you can succinctly describe the skills and experience you have in this field. A couple of well-thought-out statements should be able to get the key points across.

Then, ask this person what you want them to do for you. Maybe you want to use her name as a referral. Maybe you want to ask her to make a call to a specific person and give you an opening. Whatever it is, ask. People love to help, but they need to know what it is you want them to do. It can be hard to ask sometimes, but even if a person can't help you personally, more than likely he or she will give you the name of someone who can.

INFORMATIONAL INTERVIEWS/DIRECT CONTACT

Informational interviews are a segment of networking. You may have conducted a few when you were gathering information to narrow down your job focus. Now that you have your sights set on a specific career or job, informational interviews can help you make contact with key people, learn about possible openings, and sell what you have to offer to potential employers.

By talking with people within your field of interest and doing Internet research about different companies—their mission, environment, growth potential—you will be able to get a good sense of which companies might be a good match for you. Once you have your list, then you can start scheduling informational interviews with specific people within those organizations.

Your goal with these interviews will be different from those you did when you were gathering data about different career possibilities. You will want to get much more specific information, such as what it is like to work at a certain company or what salary range one should expect at your level of experience. Therefore, it is important to make sure the questions you ask will elicit the information you want, as well as leave a very positive impression on the person you are talking with.

INTERNET

The Internet is a great resource for the job search. You can research potential employers and specific organizations and access on-line job ads from around the world, around the country, or in your own backyard. Numerous sites will allow you to distribute your resume to potential employers. Because it is so easy and so impersonal, it can be tempting to just send out your resumes online and call it a day. But a resume is just a simple document. It is not going to sell you as well as you can sell yourself. So, send out as many resumes as you wish, but then get back and do your person-to-person networking.

NEWSPAPERS

The employment section of the want ads is the classic place to look for potential jobs. However, now that you know only 20 percent of available jobs are actually listed, this might not be the place you want to spend a great deal of your time and energy. But, as with the Internet, it won't hurt to send out your resume in response to an interesting ad. Just don't let that be your only approach.

Having said all that, the newspaper can still be a good resource. You can find articles in the business section about organizations that are expanding and businesses that have gotten new contracts. You can also find names of people who have been recently hired by different companies and who may serve as a good contact people for you. Keeping your eyes open and allowing yourself to think creatively will greatly enhance your job search.

COLLEGE CAREER CENTER

One of the best resources for career development is your college career center. Most career centers are available year-round and offer students and graduates a wide variety of career development services. These can include:

- Assessment tools to help you identify your skills, talents, and passions
- Resume, cover letter, and job search assistance
- Assistance securing part-time or full-time employment
- Opportunities for internships and volunteer work
- Current job listings from business, private industry, state and federal agencies
- Internet resources
- Annual job and career fairs
- Alumni gatherings and networking events
- Assistance with career transitions

The important thing to remember as you conduct your job search is to be organized, persistent, and believe in yourself. Keep to your time schedule. Don't give up no matter what, because you never know what might come from that one last phone call or interview. Know that you have a lot to offer and don't be afraid to strut your stuff.

Overcoming Common Obstacles

No matter how much research you do and how well you prepare, you are bound to experience some obstacles along the way. You are making a big change in your life, and with all change comes some resistance. It is the law of nature.

Resistance wants you to keep your life exactly the way it is, and it will use a variety of techniques to ensure that you make no change in your life. Resistance can take many forms. It can show up as procrastination, self-doubt, or fear. Resistance is also very subtle in its approach. It seems to always know just how much pressure it needs to apply to make sure you will abandon this silly new idea and return to life as it was.

Resistance often starts by providing you with minor distractions, such as answering the phone and engaging in a conversation with a friend instead of calling back later, and then moves on to plain old procrastination. If these tactics don't get you off course, resistance will then up the ante by bringing in the voices of fear and self-doubt. At this point, it can be easy to buy into the illusion of incompetence that resistance has created and give up. But if you do that, resistance has won and you are stuck back where you started.

There is another approach. Although it is impossible to make a change without experiencing some resistance, it is certainly not impossible to work through the resistance and achieve your goals. You just need to be aware of what to look for and have strategies ready to use to overcome the pressures of resistance. The following section will give information and techniques to help you recognize and manage common forms of resistance you may encounter.

PROCRASTINATION

Procrastination is one of the most common forms of resistance. Let's say that you had a list of three people to call for informational interviews. You sit down to make the calls, but decide that you should check your email first. As you are checking your email, you remember that you need to transfer some money into your checking account. So, after reading your emails, you go online and take care of your banking. You then return to the task of calling and your phone rings. It's a friend who has just returned from a wonderful trip, so you talk for awhile and catch up on everything she's been doing. After you hang up, you realize that you have a few minutes before your next meeting, so you decide to do the calls tomorrow.

This is a subtle version of resistance. You can easily rationalize why you didn't get to the calls. You had other things that needed to be taken care of. But if you look at the incident more closely, the real issue is what caused you to divert your attention from the calls to checking your email in the first place. You were experiencing resistance in its more subtle form. It was sending out just enough fear, doubt, or anxiety to cause you to divert your attention to something easier and more comfortable for you to do.

If you are not aware of what happened, you are likely to think that you just got distracted. You couldn't really help it if your friend called, right? But there will always be things to distract you from moving forward into new and uncharted waters. If you know what to look for, you will not be as easily diverted.

SELF-DOUBT

Let's say that you didn't fall prey to the subtle tactics. You made your calls and scheduled the interviews. Resistance is now going to crank it up a notch because you are moving too fast. This is where you might begin to hear critical voices in your head saying things like, "Why are you even doing this interview? This is a waste of time. You will never get hired."

These voices can be very persuasive and the louder they become, the more fear you feel, and the harder it is to keep moving forward. The first step to not being manipulated by these voices is to be aware of them. Notice how often voices pop up in your head to tell you that you are not good enough, smart enough, or strong enough to do whatever it is you want; and how easy it can be to accept the judgments of these voices as fact.

But they are not your true voice. They are coming from the very small part of you that doesn't want to change, and they are doing everything in their power to keep you from moving forward. When you find yourself believing what the voices are saying, don't try to argue with them. They will always win!

Instead, take a few minutes to sit quietly by yourself and try to reconnect with the part of you who has the dream, who wants to try something different, and who has the courage to step outside the box and explore new lands. This is where you will find your power. The critical voices will still play their same old tune. But the more you are able to draw upon the feelings of excitement, energy, and adventure that propelled you toward this change, the less influence those voices will have.

FEAR

Fear is another form of resistance. Fear causes you to question your abilities. You begin to worry about the decisions you are making. You find yourself obsessing about what will happen if:

- You make the wrong decision
- You can't do this
- Something better comes along
- You make a mistake

You begin mentally pacing back and forth between your options, worrying about the future effects of a decision you haven't even made yet. You are focused so intensely on the future that you can't see the opportunities that are in front of you right now. You are totally frozen in indecision. The system is happy because you are no longer in change mode, but you are left feeling unhappy and discouraged because the only decision you were able to make was not to make any decision.

Once again, the first step to avoiding this trap is to recognize when you start to get caught up in the *what-if* scenario. When you notice it happening, take a minute and see if you can identify the specific fear or doubt that is underneath. For example, you might be afraid of hurting someone's feelings. Once you realize what the issue is, you can bring it out in the open and deal with it. These kinds of fears and uncertainties only keep you stuck when they reside in the recesses of your mind. But when they are brought out into the open, they lose their power and you are free to get on with your life.

Fear is a powerful and uncomfortable emotion that can easily slip into your life and take control over what you do and don't do. The important thing to understand about fear is that it is future-based. It gains its power when you begin creating scenarios about what might happen in the future.

If you keep your focus on what's happening now, fear will have nothing to attach itself to because, at the moment, all is fine. It's only when you begin thinking about the what-ifs of the future that fear can exist. As Mark Twain so succinctly stated, "I have spent most of my life worrying about things that have never happened."

Focus and Motivation

There are many opportunities to get pulled off course in your career development process. It can be very easy to fall victim to the subtle tricks of resistance and let the fears and anxieties of an uncertain future convince you that what you are doing is too hard. But there are steps you can take to make sure that you don't let resistance and fear get in the way of you achieving your goal.

YOUR SUPPORT SYSTEM

Many of us have been raised to believe that we should be self-sufficient and able to handle whatever comes our way all by ourselves—that asking for help is not only being selfish, but is a sign of weakness. Nothing could be further from the truth. You will need the help and support of many other people if you are going to be successful and reach your goals.

Who will you call when you are feeling stuck, discouraged, or want to give up? Who will you celebrate with when you are asked in for an interview or offered a job? Who will be there to prod you, encourage you, and remind you how great you are and that what you are doing is exciting and courageous? And who will you turn to when you need information, resources, or a new perspective?

Developing this kind of safety net enables you to share the burden of your career search with others and lightens your load. It also helps ensure success, as a team effort is often more successful than a solo performance. But it can be easy to resist putting a support system into place. It might be uncomfortable for you to appear vulnerable and ask for help. It can also be a little scary to publicize your dreams. When you ask someone to help you achieve your goals, they then know what you are planning to do. What if you fall short? What if you fall flat on your face? What will they think?

There is always a slight chance that the people in your support network may have some judgments about what you do or don't do. But most people are actually their own worst critics. Having a group of people behind you who truly believe in you and what you are doing is a great way to alleviate those imagined fears and concerns.

Sometimes the people who can be the most supportive of you are people who have similar goals or who are going through a similar experience. So, you may discover that you can find a lot of support by attending workshops, seminars, or classes pertaining to your particular field of interest. If you want to find out more about the financial services field, attending an introductory seminar would not only give you the information you need, but it would also allow you to meet other people thinking about transitioning to the same field. Or if you are starting your own business and want to learn more about marketing, taking a marketing class for small businesses would introduce you to marketing ideas and other people starting up businesses.

There are a great many people and places that you can turn to for the help, support, and resources you need to keep moving forward. However, support rarely seeks you out. It will be up to you to constantly monitor your needs and actively pursue the support you need.

Finding the ideal job takes a lot of work, a lot of energy, and a great deal of support. Ask for the support you need. Don't let yourself fall short because of some outdated and inaccurate beliefs. You deserve to reach your dream.

WORKING WITH A PROFESSIONAL

You might consider hiring a professional to help facilitate your transition. Depending on your particular needs, you could choose to work with either a life coach or a career counselor. These are professionals trained to help you clarify your career goals, create and implement action plans, and develop new practices and behaviors. They can also provide the support, resources, and accountability that will ensure that you reach your stated goal.

If you decide to work with any professional, it is a good idea to interview at least three candidates so that you can find the best fit for you. Think carefully about what you are looking for in a coach or counselor. Write out a list of questions to ask so that you will be sure to get all the information you need. You would probably want to know about his or her training and experience. You might want to know if the coach has any particular methodology and what kinds of success she's had with her clients. You also need to pay attention to how you feel when you are talking to the person. Do you feel that you connect? Does the person have a sense of humor? Do you feel that he understands you?

These are the intangible qualities that can make the real difference in a relationship. Not all professionals are a good fit for everyone. To ensure the success of your coaching experience, you need to make sure that you choose the person you feel most comfortable with.

BELIEVING IN YOURSELF

The path of change is often bumpy. There will be times when you will hit walls and want to give up. There will be times when you will wonder what in the world you are doing. And there will be times when the light at the end of the tunnel will disappear and you will seriously think about turning back. But if deep in your heart you honestly believe you can reach your goal, you will most likely reach it.

Believing in yourself does not mean you will not have moments of doubt. It just means that when you do experience a breakdown, or find your motivation waning, you will be able to draw on your basic belief in yourself to pull you out of the slump and get yourself moving forward again.

But believing in yourself is not always as easy as it should be because life is constantly throwing things your way that challenge that belief. You probably have accumulated a lot of negative messages during your lifetime, many of which you have come to believe are true. You maybe have experienced previous failures and hold those as proof that you are likely to fail again. You might have people in your life who are questioning your ability to succeed.

All this negativity can easily take you away from your center—and it is when you lose your center that you will begin to question whether or not you can succeed. So, when you begin to doubt your decisions, your abilities, or your goals, take some time to sit quietly by yourself and reconnect with why you are making this change. Get in touch with the part of you that is excited, creative, and knows that there is something bigger and better waiting for you. Tap into that positive energy and you will automatically be returned to your center—the place from which you can truly be successful in finding and securing your ideal job.

For Your Reference

Books

Internet Resources

WetFeet Resources

Books

The Authentic Career
(Maggie Craddock, New World Library, 2004)

This is a wonderful book for anyone who wants to find a rewarding and meaningful career. The author gently guides you through a four-step program of questions and exercises to help you rediscover your personal strengths, accomplishments, and hidden talents so that you are better able to identify your authentic career.

The Career Adventure
(Susan M. Johnston, Prentice Hall, 2002)

This book takes the reader through a career development process that includes self-assessment, career exploration, and the job campaign. Johnston skillfully combines information, exercises, and case studies in an easy-to-read and engaging format to help the reader successfully navigate the process of finding a rewarding and fulfilling career.

Character and Personality Type:
Discovering Your Uniqueness for Career and Relationship Success
(Dario Nardi, Telos Publications, 1999)

This book provides readers with a brief overview of temperament, an interactive process to better understand themselves and others, and a short summary of the 16 type patterns of the Myers-Briggs Trait Inventory. The author takes complex information and puts it in a format that is easy to read and understand.

A Foot in the Door: Networking Your Way into the Hidden Job Market
(Katharine Hansen, Ten Speed Press, 2000)

This is the nuts-and-bolts book of effective networking. The author maps out a clear, practical approach to networking that will work for anyone. This is an essential read for anyone in the job market.

Finding a Career That Works for You:
A Step-by-Step Guide to Choosing a Career and Finding a Job
(Wilma Fellman, Specialty Press, 2000)

Finding a good career match is a complex process, but Wilma Fellman does a great job of focusing on the important issues by laying out a clear process to help you find a career that truly fits who you are, how you think, and what you want.

The Pathfinder: How to Choose or Change Your Career
for a Lifetime of Satisfaction and Success
(Nicholas Lore, Simon & Schuster, 1998)

Nicholas Lore, founder of the Rockport Institute, provides an in-depth, yet easy strategy to follow for designing the career of your dreams.

Understanding Yourself and Others, An Introduction to Temperament - 2.0
(Linda V. Berens, Telos Publications, 2000)

The personality type code devised by Isabel Myers (Myers-Briggs) is a powerful tool for explaining individual differences. This book takes a close look at the 16 personality types. It explores the whole range of cognitive processes available for accessing, gathering, and evaluating information. It also helps you see how these processes play out in your personality in both positive and negative ways.

What Type Am I?: The Myers-Briggs Type Indicator Made Easy
(Renee Baron, Penguin, 1998)

Family therapist Renee Baron explains the ideas of the Myers-Briggs Type Indicator in a way that is entertaining and easy to absorb. Readers can take the quizzes in the book to find their own type and then read full descriptions of their personalities, which also include tips for getting along gracefully in the world and finding a satisfying career.

Zen and the Art of Making a Living: A Practical Guide to Creative Career Design
(Laurence G. Bolt, The Penguin Group, 1993)

This book combines traditional career information such as identifying skills, decision-making, networking, and resume writing with the larger quest of finding personal and spiritual fulfillment through your work. The book also offers information not always found in career books, including how to start a business, working freelance, establishing nonprofits, and managing multiple careers. This book goes far beyond the average career guide in helping you broaden your perspective and finding your ideal career.

Internet Resources

Here are sites where you can find the online version of some of the reference guides mentioned in "Exploring Your Career Landscape."

O*NET (www.onecenter.org)
This is the online version of the *Dictionary of Occupational Titles.*

Occupational Outlook Handbook (www.bls.gov/oco/)

The following websites provide information regarding personality assessment tools. Some offer free online tests.

Careers By Design (www.careers-by-design.com)

The Enneagram Institute (www.enneagraminstitute.com)

Holland Occupational Theme Exercise (www.soicc.state.nc.us/soicc/planning/c1a.htm)

Holland Self-Directed Search® (www.self-directed-search.com)

Keirsey.com (www.keirsey.com)

The Personality Page (www.personalitypage.com)

similarminds.com (www.similarminds.com)

TypeLogic.com (www.typelogic.com)

ADDITIONAL SITES

America's Job Bank (www.ajb.dni.us/)
This is a partnership between the U.S. Department of Labor and the Public Employment Service.

U.S. Equal Employment Opportunity Commission (www.eeoc.gov)
This is the federal agency in charge of the administrative and judicial enforcement of the federal civil rights laws.

WetFeet Resources

The following WetFeet titles are available at www.WetFeet.com and www.Amazon.com. See the last two pages of this Insider Guide for a complete list of WetFeet books.

Ace Your Interview!

Interviewing is the most important job-seeking skill and the one barrier that every job seeker must face before getting hired. But it doesn't have to be a harrowing experience. At its core, a job interview is really just a specific kind of conversation. This book, complete with sample interview scripts and workbooks, will help you make the preparations necessary to keep that conversation focused, productive, and pleasant, so that you can keep your wits about you even when the stakes seem alarmingly high.

Changing Course, Changing Careers

Dread going to work every day? Exhausted by the prospect of another year doing the same thing? Craving a career that energizes you? Sounds like you know it's time to change the course of your life. Chances are you just don't know how. Fortunately, WetFeet has tapped career transitions expert Mary Ann Bailey to help you navigate the murky waters of career change. Mary Ann has helped many dissatisfied professionals identify the career best for them, gather the courage to pursue their dreams, and develop a step-by-step plan for making their dreams a reality. With this book, Mary Ann can do the same for you.

Job Hunting A to Z: Landing the Job You Want

Networking, interviewing, and negotiating are key steps in securing your ideal job—learn to do them well, and you'll have a foothold on a brilliant career. In this WetFeet Insider Guide, Robert A. Fish, founder of Right Management Consultants, the largest outplacement consulting firm in the United States, sets out clear and easy-to-follow advice for landing the job you want.

Killer Cover Letters and Resumes!

Your objective: Stand out from the pack. Thanks to the ease of submitting a resume online, recruiters today receive literally hundreds of resumes for each open position. How do they sift through these stacks of resumes? What can you do to position yourself at the top of the heap? In this WetFeet Insider Guide, career advisor Rosanne Lurie explores these questions to bring you the latest wisdom from recruiters and hiring managers.

Negotiating Your Salary and Perks

Whether facing your first salary negotiation or your tenth, you will fare much better if you have some basic negotiation skills. In fact, almost every initial offer can be improved on—in many cases, dramatically—with a little savvy negotiating. In this WetFeet Insider Guide, Duncan Haberly, Esq., and Robert Fish, Phd., give you the tools to maximize your salary, title, responsibilities, perks, work flexibility, and more by teaching you how to negotiate the terms of your next job from the moment you start looking for it.

Networking Works!

Most job vacancies are filled well before a job description is posted. How do people know about these secret openings? That's right—networking! Don't worry: Networking isn't as mysterious as it seems. In fact, most of us already engage in personal networking all the time. Ever asked your friends for a recommendation for a hairdresser or auto mechanic? Guess what? You're networking, baby! This book will show you how to network effectively for professional development, even if you don't know where to start.

About the Author

Mary Ann Bailey, M.C., is a life coach who specializes in working with people going through career transitions.

Mary Ann's expertise in career transition is a combination of personal and professional experience. She started her career path in the field of education, teaching junior high and high school for 10 years before deciding to change careers. She returned to school and received a master's degree in counseling. Upon completing her counseling internship, she was hired as a youth and family counselor at a mental health agency, where she stayed for 4 years doing direct service work before earning the opportunity to move into the role of program director. Three years later she was promoted to associate director of the agency.

After working for 12 years in the nonprofit sector, Mary Ann decided it was once again time for a career change. At this point in her life, her priorities had changed. She wanted to do something that was more personally fulfilling, something that combined her strongest skills with her deepest passion, and something that gave her greater flexibility in her work schedule. Coaching seemed like the perfect answer. She started her own coaching business, Bailey Coaching, and has helped people from all walks of life transition to more personally satisfying and rewarding careers.

Mary Ann holds a BA in psychology, a master's in counseling, and is a graduate of the Integral Coaching Program of New Ventures West in San Francisco. She is a member of the International Coach Federation and the Puget Sound Coaches Association. She is also the author of the WetFeet Insider Guide *Changing Course, Changing Careers*. For more information about Mary Ann, visit her web site at www.BaileyCoaching.com.

WETFEET'S INSIDER GUIDE SERIES

Job Search Guides
Getting Your Ideal Internship
International MBA Student's Guide to the U.S. Job Search
Job Hunting A to Z: Landing the Job You Want
Killer Consulting Resumes!
Killer Cover Letters & Resumes!
Killer Investment Banking Resumes!
Negotiating Your Salary & Perks
Networking Works!

Interview Guides
Ace Your Case: Consulting Interviews
Ace Your Case II: 15 More Consulting Cases
Ace Your Case III: Practice Makes Perfect
Ace Your Case IV: The Latest & Greatest
Ace Your Case V: Return to the Case Interview
Ace Your Case VI: Mastering the Case Interview
Ace Your Interview!
Beat the Street: Investment Banking Interviews
Beat the Street II: I-Banking Interview Practice Guide

Career & Industry Guides
Careers in Accounting
Careers in Advertising & Public Relations
Careers in Asset Management & Retail Brokerage
Careers in Biotech & Pharmaceuticals
Careers in Brand Management
Careers in Consumer Products
Careers in Entertainment & Sports
Careers in Health Care
Careers in Human Resources
Careers in Information Technology

Careers in Investment Banking
Careers in Management Consulting
Careers in Marketing & Market Research
Careers in Nonprofits & Government Agencies
Careers in Real Estate
Careers in Retail
Careers in Sales
Careers in Supply Chain Management
Careers in Venture Capital
Industries & Careers for MBAs
Industries & Careers for Undergrads
Million Dollar Careers
Specialized Consulting Careers: Health Care, Human Resources, and Information Technology

Company Guides

25 Top Consulting Firms
25 Top Financial Services Firms
Accenture
Bain & Company
Booz Allen Hamilton
Boston Consulting Group
Credit Suisse First Boston
Deloitte Consulting
Deutsche Bank
The Goldman Sachs Group
J.P. Morgan Chase & Co.
McKinsey & Company
Merrill Lynch & Co.
Morgan Stanley

WetFeet in the City Guides

Job Hunting in New York City
Job Hunting in San Francisco